Uniforms & Equipment of the Imperial German Army 1900-1918

VOLUME 2

Uniforms & Equipment of the Imperial German Army 1900-1918 VOLUME 2

A Study in Period Photographs
AIR SERVICE • CAVALRY • ASSAULT TROOPS •
SIGNAL TROOPS • PICKELHAUBEN • STEEL HELMETS •
VEHICLES •

Charles Woolley

Schiffer Military History
Atglen, PA

ACKNOWLEDGMENTS

With this, the second volume of the series, I must again applaud the efforts made by Captain Tony Meldahl, who while serving in the United States Army stationed in Germany, built this collection of wonderful photographs, choosing only the best after sorting through thousands of available images.

Kudos to Bill Shea, dear friend and, in my opinion, the best, most straight-forward militaria dealer in the trade today. He obtained the collection from Tony, kept it together, and has shared it with all to enjoy through these volumes. Thanks for so many things Bill!

Finally, my deepest thanks to my wife Nancy who continues to master foreign military words and phrases which make up many of the captions seen here, enters all into the computer, puts them into a readable format, makes me edit everything with care, and, therefore, through her efforts, the publishing of this book is possible.

As in volume one, all the original photographs used are available for purchase. For further information, you may contact the author through e-mail: woolley@sover.net.

Book design by Robert Biondi.

Copyright © 2000 by Charles Woolley.
Library of Congress Catalog Number: 99-61652.

All rights reserved. No part of this work may be reproduced or used in any forms or by any means – graphic, electronic or mechanical, including photocopying or information storage and retrieval systems – without written permission from the copyright holder.

"Schiffer," "Schiffer Publishing Ltd. & Design," and the "Design of pen and ink well" are registered trademarks of Schiffer Publishing, Ltd.

Printed in China.
ISBN: 0-7643-1104-2

We are interested in hearing from authors with book ideas on related topics.

Published by Schiffer Publishing Ltd.
4880 Lower Valley Road
Atglen, PA 19310
Phone: (610) 593-1777
FAX: (610) 593-2002
E-mail: Schifferbk@aol.com.
Visit our web site at: www.schifferbooks.com
Please write for a free catalog.
This book may be purchased from the publisher.
Please include $3.95 postage.
Try your bookstore first.

In Europe, Schiffer books are distributed by:
Bushwood Books
6 Marksbury Road
Kew Gardens
Surrey TW9 4JF
England
Phone: 44 (0)181 392-8585
FAX: 44 (0)181 392-9876
E-mail: Bushwd@aol.com.

Try your bookstore first.

Contents

Chapter One	The Photographs	6
	Machine Gun Troops	7
	Assault Troops and Grenades	36
	Swords, Bayonets and Trench Weapons	50
	M1895 Blue Uniform	61
	Minenwerfer (Mortars) and Crews	70
	Stahlhelm - Steel Helmets	87
	Decorative Steins, Pipes and Patriotic Items	95
	Telegraph and Signal Troops	110
	Field Artillery Personnel	113
	Kraftfahrer, Motordrivers and Vehicles	129
	Ersatz Pickelhauben M1915	135
	Cavalry: Dragoons	146
	Bavarian Chavaulegers	151
	Jäger zu Pferde	157
	Ulans	159
	Kürassiere	175
	Husaren	181
	Railroad - Eisenbahn Troops	195
	Anti-Aircraft Artillery	199
	Air Service	203
	Commissary	245
	Heavy Artillery	255
	Horses and Pets	262
	Pickelhauben in Detail	269
Chapter Two	Color Section	284
	Glossary	309
	Further Reading	311

Chapter One

The Photographs

Volume Two of *Uniforms & Equipment of the Imperial German Army 1900-1918* continues the photographic study begun in Volume I, expanding into additional branches and equipment not covered before. The source of the original photographs reproduced here are, as before, primarily from the collection amassed by Tony Meldahl, with additions from the collection of the author.

The reader will find the Imperial Air Service section contains primarily photographs of personnel, and not an abundance of aircraft views which would, in themselves, create a volume. The Sanke cards of the leading decorated Imperial Air Service personnel are but a sampling of the large number published during the war, and which constitutes a field of collecting of its own.

The captions have been researched as thoroughly as possible; a bibliography of sources is included, but surely an eagle-eyed expert may find an exception or a detail unmentioned, of which the author would like to be made aware. This may be done through the publisher, and will be corrected in the next volume.

One of the great pleasures to be obtained from the study of period photographs is the discovery of little details which have not been seen before, or widely publicized. The reader is urged to take advantage of these pleasures and carefully study the photographs. As shown in them, one may be amazed by the liberties taken by the German front-line soldiers, as well as officers, in their interpretation of the regulations concerning dress and equipment. As a result, we collectors must take care in the insistence, "It can't be right because it's out of the nine dots of the regulations." (An outline of the regulations appears in volume one.) Individuality and personal indifference to what was prescribed did take place in the Imperial German Army of 1900-1918, in spite of the iron fist of Prussian authority and all of its perceived inflexibility.

Machine Gun Troops

A training photo of a Saxon MG 08 crew wearing M1895 blue uniforms with "12" on the shoulder straps, and uncovered M1915 pickelhaube helmets. The gun is the standard Maxim design MG 08 and the ammunition box is the M1911 Patronenkaste II which is twin-sectioned holding two belts of 250 rounds each.

A gun crew of Saxon Grenadier Regiment Nr. 101 in training under the watchful eye of an NCO wearing a visor cap in the center of the photo. Three men wear the gun dragging straps over their shoulders, the double ammunition box and the cylindrical water can with its carrying handle upright are seen in the foreground.

A photography studio has gone to considerable trouble to erect this backdrop in an outdoor setting. The MG 08 gun crew are from Infantry Regiment Nr. 180 wearing a mix of M1910 and M1915 uniforms. Four men are equipped with leather dragging straps, one poses with a Pionier shovel, while the others are at their stations. Interestingly, the gun has the blank firing attachment on the muzzle and the cartridges in the belt appear to be blanks. The date of the Feldpost stamp is 23 September 1917.

The five-men crew of this MG 08 have placed the legs of the sled mount in their lowest prone position. The men are attached to Infantry Regiment Nr. 35 and the photographer is from Brandenburg. This was a posed photo as there is no water cooling can evident, nor are the barrel booster and flash hider in position in this 16 March 1917 dated photograph.

The twelve men in this photo have the look of seasoned troops. They wear a mix of M1910 and M1915 uniforms adorned with Iron Cross 2nd Class ribbons and the NCO in the center has been awarded a black wound badge. In the left foreground are four of the single belt Patronenkaste 15 which were carried in pairs, and on the right, the rectangular steam condensing can which saw service in the mid and late war.

The oval plate on the wall proclaims this group to be from the 9. Komp - LIR 119 (Landwehr Infantry Regiment 119). They were near the front as the MG 08 wears two of the four pieces of armor designed for machine gun use. In view are the Water Jacket Front Shield by the muzzle and the Water Jacket Top Shield covering the top and sides of the vulnerable water jacket. The Feldpost stamp shows a date of 5 September 1916.

On 26 January 1917 Festungs Machine Gewehr Kompanie 6 posed in the snow for this picture. This was a Landsturm outfit with the Arabic numeral "7" on their collars. The gun on the left carries the Water Jacket Front Shield and both are equipped with the earlier style cylindrical steam condenser can with their hoses attached. Eight of the double Patronenkaste II ammunition boxes are in the foreground.

The legs of the sled mount of this MG 08 are in the fully extended prone firing position. The flash hider, the cone-shaped piece and the flash protector, and the circular piece, are seen at the muzzle of the gun. The gunners were from Infantry Regiment Nr. 127 and appear to be in training.

As the war became more static, Cavalry regiments became specialized ground troops. Here we see Husars serving as a machine gun crew. The man on the left is wearing a Husar attila, or frogged jacket, leg wraps, and an M1916 steel helmet. The open claw cavalry-style belt can be seen on the man observing on the right. The round flash protector is clearly shown on the gun, as is the rubber steam hose.

A five-man machine gun crew of Infantry Regiment Nr. 149 posed for this photograph on 1 January 1916. The background building and the newness of their M1910 uniforms would make one think that these men had recently completed their training. The MG 08 is in an interesting position of full leg elevation of the mount, and full depression of the gun which shows the ribbed undersides of this style mount in contrast to the mount in the preceding photograph.

Oscar Hepperlin was the photographer at Lager Hammelburg where Bavarian Infantry Regiment Nr. 12 was receiving its machine gun training. The crewman on the far right displays the 1913 Koenigspreis marksman's badge in an unusual feldgrau backing. The MG 08 is equipped with the Zielfernrohr 12 (ZF 12) optic sight and the spotter has a pair of Fernglas 08 binoculars. Four double Patronenkaste II ammunition boxes are on the left and the steam/water hose is being held by the spotter.

A wonderful photograph dated 12 April 1918 shows two machine gun crews from the Garde Ulan regiment wearing their ulankas and ersatz felt Ulan helmets. The Patronenkaste II and cylindrical steam condenser cans can be seen in this garrison sited view.

Eighteen young trainees from Württemberg Infantry Regiment Nr. 180 pose with their NCO instructors, in the center rear, who display their Iron Cross ribbons on their M1915 blusen. Both machine guns are equipped with the blank ammunition muzzle attachments, Patronenkaste 15 single belt boxes and cylindrical steam condensing cans. The date of the card is 15 September 1918, which seems late for the issuance of M1910 tunics to these recruits.

Six members of one of the Machine Gewehr Kompanie of Infantry Regiment Nr. 114 pose with their MG 08. Live ammunition is being fed to the gun from a Patronenkaste 15 and a cylindrical water can is on the right. Four of the men are equipped with the later style dragging harnesses made of webbing rather than leather, and the gun has both the flash hider and flash shield.

The 1917 date of this photograph is marked on the Schild 08, or the standard MG 08 armor shield. The crew of this gun are with Infantry Regiment Nr. 59, armed with P. 08 Lugers and dressed in M1910 uniforms, with the exception of the decorated NCO in an M1915 Bluse. The gun is equipped with a ZF 12 optic sight and a muzzle attachment for firing blanks. This was a picture taken during the training process.

November 11, 1916 is the date on the reverse of this posed picture. The crew is from Saxon Infantry Regiment Nr. 104 and are wearing their pre-war style overcoats with the regimental cyphered shoulder straps. The belt being fed to the gun is empty of ammunition, while an excellent view is provided of the top of the steam condensing can showing the spigot for returning water to the gun and the folding carrying handle.

A superb photograph of 26 members of the Machinen Gewehr Kompanie of Grenadier-Regiment "Königin Olga" (1. Württ.) Nr. 119. Careful inspection of this picture shows two MG 08 guns, Kar 98a's, a field telephone, a range finder on its tripod, dragging harnesses, P. 08 Lugers, 6 NCOs and a decorated officer. The regimental "Crown over O" cyphered shoulder straps are visible on many of the M1910 uniform tunics in this really detailed and unique picture.

Two machine gun transport wagons and guns with a mounted officer and drivers stand before their crews of Infantry Regiment Nr. 147. Note the happy young man by the near wagon wearing a boy's visor cap and an issue belt and buckle supporting a small pouch. A most unusual photograph.

A Maschinengewehr crew pose indoors in their newly issued M1915 uniforms. In the picture are seen four spikeless M1915 pickelhauben, leather dragging harnesses, M1915 Gummimask gas masks, two double Patronenkaste II ammunition boxes, and a small leather-cased toolkit. The card is dated 12 August 1917, and the Feldpost stamp is marked Inf. Masch.-Gew.-Ausb.-Kdo.

The thirteen men in this photograph appear to be well-seasoned veterans. Bravery award ribbons are displayed on well-worn M1910 tunics, some of which have been replaced by the M1915 Bluse. The date on the reverse is 28 July 1918. The regiment is not identified, but "MGK 19" appears below the date.

Uniforms and Equipment of the Imperial German Army 1900-1918

Thirteen members of Württemberg Infantry Regiment 120 pose in a rustic setting with an MG 08 Maxim in the foreground. The photograph was taken near the lines, as the gun wears its armor cover over the front of the water jacket. A variety of M1910 and M1915 uniforms are seen with leg-wraps and boots being worn. The NCO in the center has been awarded the Iron Cross 2nd Class.

Dismounted members of Württemberg Dragoon Regiment 26 pose with an MG 08 on the Vogesen Front, France 1917-18. They have been assigned as "Kavalerie Schützen MG Truppen". The NCO on the left has been awarded fencing proficiency chevrons and wears the crown and W cypher of the regiment on his shoulder straps.

Anti-aircraft work was the role of this MG 08 team from Infantry Iregiment Nr. 132. The optic sight and frontal armor can be seen on the gun. Two variants of the leather drag harnesses are being worn, as well as P. 08 Luger sidearms. The NCO has been awarded both classes of the Iron Cross.

Uniforms and Equipment of the Imperial German Army 1900-1918

An MG 08 mounted on one of the variety of trench mounts which were put into service prior to availability of the lighter MG 08/15. This mount was used for anti-aircraft purposes and the NCO on the right wears the insignia of a FLAMGA, or Flak Machine Gewehr Abteilung. Model 1910 and 1915 tunics and blouses are worn, a telegrapher's belt buckle supports the belt and pistol of the man behind the gun, and gas mask containers indicate a forward position of this team.

A crew of Naval infantry from the 2 Matrossen Regiment in Flanders. The MG 08 is mounted on the Naval style mount and the crew is equipped with the early rare cloth gas masks suspended on their shoulders.

Three machine gun troopers have finished training and are ready for departure to the front. They are all equipped with the leather dragging harnesses, trench flashlights, and armed with Mauser M96 pistols in their wooden shoulder stock holsters. The man on the left who appears to be wearing a tunic of the Grengrau material for Jägers and MG Truppen carries a small entrenching tool or shovel, initially issued to MG troops.

A young, recently trained, Bavarian machine gun trooper poses in his new equipment before heading to the front. He is wearing an M1915 pickelhaube with the Bavarian frontplate and is armed with a P. 08 Luger and a short S71/84 bayonet. The Feldpost stamp on the reverse is dated January 18, 1916.

A formal studio photograph of a Bavarian MG Scharfschützen Unteroffizier. Of interest are his Bavarian M1916 Feldbluse with the special Bavarian borte collar trim, 2nd Class Iron Cross ribbon, machine gun sharpshooter's sleeve badge, open-style belt buckle and the S71/84 short bayonet with troddel identifying his company.

A senior Bavarian NCO of 2 Machine Gewehr Scharfschützen, Abteilung 3. He is wearing a private purchase uniform and visor cap, as well as an M1909 feldgrau mounted troops overcoat with the machine gun Scharfschützen badge on the sleeve. The Feldpost stamp on the reverse is dated 12 March 1917.

A group of decorated men and NCOs from the 6th Machine Gun Company of Reserve Infantry Regiment 249. They are all wearing the M1910 and M1910/15 tunics and the NCO center row right has a crown and cypher on his shoulder straps. RIR249 was part of the 75th Reserve division and the divisional Feldpost stamp bears the date August 9, 1916.

Twelve members of Infantry Regiment 123 strike a war-like pose with an MG 08/15, Patronenkasten 15 ammo boxes, what may be a Gurtfuller 16 belt filling machine in the light colored wooden box, hand grenades and gas mask carriers. Of interest in the left background are two sets of sentry's body armor.

Uniforms and Equipment of the Imperial German Army 1900-1918

A photograph of an MG 05/15 crew with much interesting detail. At least three of the crew are armed with small Mauser M1910 automatics, and three have what appears to be web dragging straps over their shoulders, but not necessary with an 08/15. The canvas toolkit is unrolled by the kneeling man on the left, the single belt Patronenkaste 15 is feeding the gun, and the steam condenser hose disappears on the left of the photo. M1910 and M1915 uniforms, leg-wraps, and Fernglas 08 binoculars complete the picture.

An MG 08/15 is being served by a crew wearing M1916 Stalhelms camouflaged in several different patterns. The man on the left wears the ribbon of the Iron Cross 2nd Class, a holstered P. 08 Luger, and has his gas mask at the ready. The large box on the left is in all probability the machine gun toolbox and three Patronenkasten 15 single belt ammo boxes are evident.

This photo, mailed 30 March 1915 from Nürnberg, shows an Ersatz Machine-Gewehr Kompanie outside the Kaserne having completed their training and preparing for the front. They wear M1909 overcoats for mounted troops, pickelhauben with field covers, slings, short bayonets, and a variety of flashlights.

A six-man MG 08/15 crew wearing the M1915 bluse, M1916 steel helmets and armed with P. 08 Lugers pose for this photograph dated on the reverse 23 January 1918. The case slung over the shoulder of the left kneeling man is unidentified.

Freiberg photographer C. Hertel took this picture of heavily armed infantrymen with a single MG 08/15. All identifying shoulder straps have been removed from the uniforms, and although there is no date on the photo, one might wonder if it might have been taken of a Freikorps group the winter after the war ended.

A three-man MG 08/15 crew prepare for action. The 100 round trommel, or drum magazine, for the MG 08/15, officially known as the Patronenkasten 16, is seen on the right side of the gun. The crewman on the left carries the steam condenser can and the hose, while the man on the right carries two Patronenkasten 15 single belt ammunition boxes. The photograph is dated 1918 on the reverse.

An MG 08/15 and crew in a forward position. No helmets are seen, indicating a lull in the action, but barbed wire entanglements can be seen in the background. From the look on the men's faces, the war was taking its toll.

An MG 08 on a trench mount assumes an anti-aircraft role. The trench has electricity as can be seen by the insulators and wire behind the crew. Camouflage has been strung over the position which must be fairly close to the front lines as the men have their gas masks slung at the ready.

The two MG Scharfschützen armed with P. 08 Lugers stand behind one of the most important machine gun accessories, the range-finder, seen here on its tripod with the carrying tube in the foreground.

A machine gunner from Füsilier Regiment Nr. 34 stands well-equipped for this photo by Emil Strobel. On his right hip he carries a Zielfernrohr 12 (ZF12) optic sight in its leather case, a P. 08 Luger on his left hip and a dragging strap for an MG 08 over his shoulder. His shoulder straps show Füsilier Regiment Nr. 34, but the Brief-stempel on the reverse states "Res. Inftr. Regt. 65 M.G.K." The Feldpost stamp states "16. Reserve Division" with the date 13 January 1916.

The youth registered in their faces, and the date of 1918, gives a clear picture of the manpower shortage of the German army. These boys of the Saxon Jäger Batallion 12 pose with two MG 08/15s and three veteran NCOs wearing the visor caps. The others wear the Saxon Shakos distinguished by their black horsehair plumes, or haarbusch.

This eager MG 08 crew are ready to take on all comers, although this is most likely a training photo as indicated by the observing NCO in the visor cap. The double Patronenkasten II is clearly shown as is the ZF 12 optic sight and the dragging straps on two crew members.

The machine gun rangefinder is clearly shown in this photograph. The carrying case for the instrument is on the back of the Bavarian operator, while the soft case for the tripod is on his left hip, and the P. 08 Luger in its holster is carried on his right.

BELOW: An early Maschinegewehr unit photo taken by Heinz Bensemann of Metz shows a Bavarian MG Abteilung equipped with the MG 01 on the early type Schlittenlafette, or sled mount. These early mounts, Schlitten 01, are identified by the large circular rings above the front legs.

Belgium was the location of the photographer who took this group shot. The two men standing on the right wear MG Scharfschützen sleeve badges, while the man lower left bears the Infanterie Regiment Nr. 38 numbers on his shoulder straps. M1910/15 and M15 uniforms are in evidence.

Two Prussian machine gun troops pose for a Loos, Belgium photographer. The unit number "230" appears on their Shako covers, as well as their shoulder straps. They are dressed in M1910 tunics and are armed with holstered pistols.

An NCO and enlisted man clad in M1910/15 tunics, visor caps, snow goggles and high snow gaiters, pose in a winter setting behind a machine gun rangefinder. The print was made from a glass negative which was cracked, as evidenced by the line in the upper right corner.

BELOW: A rather dark photo of machine gun troops and an MG 08/15 equipped with the 100-round trommel, or drum magazine. Other interesting details in the picture are the telegrapher's belt buckle on the man standing on the right, the rectangular metal carrier for two spare barrels, a single belt Patronenkaste 15, and the small round container, or soaking can, called the Petroleumbusche 08/15 S which removed the deposits left by heavy firing on the MG 08/15 ball booster, or Ruckstossverstarker 08/15 S. The reverse is dated 1917.

Austrian troops pose with the Schwarzlose M 7/12 which was used in limited quantities by the Germans. U.S. Marine Corps records show that at least one example of this Austrian made gun was captured at Belleau Wood. This card is dated 18 August 1918 on the reverse.

The Russian Maxim 1910 model with the fluted water jacket, and the Sokolov wheeled mount. The mount was heavy, about 100 pounds, and featured two forward legs which were normally folded to the rear, and the gun, when necessary, was moved by its wheels. As this photo shows, the legs could be swung forward to create a tripod; the wheels elevated off the ground. Many of these were used by German reserve and Landsturm units on the Eastern Front. The reverse of this card is Feldpost marked "Masch. Gewehr Komp Inf Reg 168" and dated August 1916.

Uniforms and Equipment of the Imperial German Army 1900-1918

A captured French St. Etienne Ml. 1907 with its ammunition box containing long fixed strips of cartridges. The reverse is dated 30 June 1916 and Feldpost stamped "Landwehr Infanterie - Regiment Nr. 121".

A captured British Class "C" Vickers in .303 caliber, mounted on a Mark IV tripod. This gun was captured 28 March 1918 in the field near Brébières, France by members of Infanterie Regiment 180, Co II.

Assault Troops and Grenades

Landsturm assault troops of the 18th Bataljon, XIII Army Corps are laden with stick grenades called "potato mashers" and display a case of egg grenades in the center foreground. The steel helmets are M16 and the uniforms M1910.

An interesting training photograph of young recruits from Füsilier Regiment Nr. 40 taken at Rastatt and mailed on 1 December 1917. Many of the recruits are dressed in the M1895 blue uniforms; the rest in M1910 tunics. An unusual detail is the evidence of square cloth patches over the numbers on the pickelhaube covers. As this is a group in training, they all are carrying the practice grenades which have drilled heads painted red, but are equipped with combat assault grenade bags.

A group photograph shows eight assault truppen, including an NCO with a holstered P. 08 Luger, and an Einjarig-freiwilliger, 2nd from the left. Most have grenades and their carrying bags slung in position, gas masks hung to the rear and M16 steel helmets. These men are from Infanterie Regiment Nr. 76 III. Batn. 9. Komp. and the Feldpost stamp bears a date of 22 July 1917.

An early war photograph which bears close study. At the far right are three unusual type grenades in view. The soldier is holding a "paddle" grenade and on the parapet are examples of the M13 serrated round grenade, one with the lanyard attached and two of the "Tortoise" offensive grenades. The rifleman behind the armored shield has his ammunition clips laid out on a cloth to protect them from dirt, while the others have bayonet's fixed, including two of the rarer Yataghan bladed versions on the left. The man in the dark overcoat and pickelhaube has a cloth bandolier slung around his neck and all wear extra protection against the cold.

Four battle hardened riflemen pose by a barn somewhere in France. They are all wearing cloth camouflage covers on their M16 steel helmets and a variety of M1910, M1910/15 and M15 uniforms. Gew 98.s and stick grenades make up their armament.

Uniforms and Equipment of the Imperial German Army 1900-1918

A Kavalerie Schützen Regiment member is ready for all contingencies. These cavalry troops have been relieved of their horses and serve as assault troops in the front lines. He is equipped with M1911 cavalry-style ammunition pouches, cavalry-style belt, an M1915 Gummimask for gas protection, two stick grenades, a Kar 98a with ersatz bayonet and an M1915 Bluse. The reverse is dated 18 March 1917.

Nine Iron Cross 2nd Class winners grace this group of infantrymen most of whom are holding practice stick grenades. A variety of M1910/15 and M1915 uniforms are being worn by the men in the photograph which is marked on the reverse "Sturm Trupp fuer den 26.7.17."

The 20th of November 1915 was the Feldpost stamp date on this photo of nine members of Bavarian Infanterie Regiment 12. They are in a well-fortified trench position with Gew 98.s and stick grenades ready to repulse any attack.

Dismounted Dragoons pose in a trench during a lull in the fighting. Two of the troopers have been awarded the Iron Cross 2nd Class and the man on the far right carries two stick grenades and has a gas mask in a canvas carrier slung over his shoulder. Plain bands cover the lower colored position of their mützen, or field caps, and Kar 98a carbines are the weapon of choice.

Members of Bavarian Infanterie Regiment Nr. 3 pose near the front lines with pipes, cigars and examples of the early paddle grenades which preceded the later stick or "potato masher" grenades. The on-duty men are wearing M1910/15 tunics, covered pickelhauben pre-war M1895 patronentaschen, or ammunition boxes, and Gew 98. rifles.

Uniforms and Equipment of the Imperial German Army 1900-1918

A late war photograph of an Assault trooper wearing an M1918 helmet, M1915 Bluse, M1909 ammunition pouches suspended by a breadbag strap, leg-wraps, armed with a Gew 98., an ersatz bayonet, and a stick grenade. A two-colored armband is worn on his lower left sleeve which may have been used to identify smaller sub-units.

Troops advancing through a gap in the barbed wire late in February 1916. The man going over-the-top has a stick grenade hung on his belt and is armed, as the others, with a Gew 98. The plain colored adjustable mütze bands are clearly seen on these troops from Landwehr Infanterie Regiment Nr. 119., 7. Komp.

A training photograph taken in October of 1917 shows a mixed group of NCOs and enlisted men attending an assault school. The trainees are wearing pickelhauben, overcoats in the assault rolled position, and are carrying practice stick grenades.

A group of Grenadiers prepared for an assault. Wearing M16 helmets, M1910/15 tunics and M1915 bluses and equipped with both leather and rubberized canvas gas masks, this veteran squad have armed themselves with copious numbers of grenades and Gew 98.s prior to a trench raid.

An NCO looks over a display of German ordnance ranging from a heavy mortar shell in the center, to hand grenades. The grenade second from the right is the unusual "Wilhelm" model steel shafted stick grenade and next to it is an example of the parachute grenade. The M18 fragmented egg grenade and the "Tortoise" offensive grenade are on the left.

A recent recipient of the Iron Cross 2nd Class poses in a state of combat readiness. An M16 helmet, M15 bluse, M1909 ammunition pouches, Gew 98. with a steel handled ersatz bayonet and a stick grenade are the various components of his equipment.

This card was mailed 1 April 1917 from the 6th Bavarian Infanterie Regiment, 2nd Maschine Gewehr Abteilung. The two happy warriors seem pleased to have made it another day and are armed for an assault. Steel helmets, grenades, gas mask containers, and Gew 98.s indicate a closeness to the front lines.

The Vogesen Front in France was the scene of this most interesting photograph. The troops seen here are from a Husar cavalry unit who are fighting as Kavallerie Schützen without horses. A close look at the picture discloses a variety of equipment and uniforms, Husar attilas, M1910, M1910/15, M1915 tunics, cloth covered steel helmets, Kar 98a carbines, a variety of grenade carriers, 1st Class Iron Crosses, fighting knives, and gas masks to name a few. The man lower right has a P. 08 stuck in his belt and overall this view is worthy of close study.

Uniforms and Equipment of the Imperial German Army 1900-1918

ABOVE: November 25, 1917 is the date of the message on the reverse of this field photograph. All eleven of these assault troops are equipped with M16 steel helmets, gas masks, grenades and Gew 98.s.

A good view of a German front-line trench and dugout. It would appear that these troops had recently repulsed a French attack as a French Adrian-style steel helmet with a Chasseur horn emblem and a horn or bugle from a Chasseur unit are being proudly displayed, as well as stick grenades of an early type. Note the barbed wire support device spanning the trench at the top of the photograph.

Fourteen helmeted trainees and two NCO instructors from the 214 Infanterie Division strike a pose. Practice grenades are in the hands of the two prone men. The date written on the reverse is 7 September 1918.

A faded but unusual photograph of Jäger troops in a defensive trench position. Their shako covers are marked "R 60", a trench sniper shield protects the nearest Jäger and early-style stick grenades are piled by the rifle position. The second Gew 98. on the firing line has its protective breech cover in position so it would seem that an immediate attack was not contemplated. Note the construction of the trench, a standing firing position with a stepped-up area in front and a lower sitting position next to stacked arms.

Uniforms and Equipment of the Imperial German Army 1900-1918

Two enlisted men and seven NCOs pose before a door which is marked to a "Schule", or school. These are combat veterans, as the majority wear the ribbon of the Iron Cross 2nd Class. The two crossed stick grenades and steel helmet have some significance, in all likelihood symbols of an assault school.

A sentry poses before a courtyard with an M16 helmet, Gew 98., two stick grenades and leg-wraps. Two other details are the lack of shoulder boards on his M15 Bluse and the officer leaning on the staff car in the courtyard. Could be a Freikorps early post-war photograph.

Swords, Bayonets and Trench Weapons

A trench club looking like a small baseball bat hangs from the wall of the trench wall on the left. The MG 08 located on the raised firing platform is protected by the water jacket armor, but is not on its mount. The wooden blocks with handles on the left have not yet been identified.

A decorated NCO Infantryman poses with a variety of shells at his feet, his Gew 98., M 09 cartridge boxes suspended by a breadbag strap and a trench fighting knife on his belt. These fighting knives were made by many companies, including Demag (Deutsche Maschinenfabrik). The average blade was 6 inches in length, and the grips were slab-sided wood with simple grooved ribs similar to the bayonets. The photo is dated April 14, 1916.

An NCO from Infantry Regiment Nr. 17 fully armed emerges from a damaged building. His uniform seems remarkably clean for a combat involved soldier, but his equipment is of interest. He wears an M16 steel helmet, a gas mask, a flashlight, an extra ammunition bandolier, a Gew 98., and a spring-loaded trench club in his right hand. This example is of English manufacture and called by the Germans "Totschläger," or death club.

Uniforms and Equipment of the Imperial German Army 1900-1918

This photograph gives us a closer view of the Totschläger trench club. The wrist thong hangs over the 15 cm projectile suspending the well-turned wooden handle, the leverage spring and the heavy hammer end. The intensity of trench fighting can be well-imagined looking at this deadly instrument. An English No. 36 MKI Mills grenade is on the left and a German fragmentation grenade on the right of the picture.

A decorated NCO in an M1910 tunic and visor cap sits casually in a dry, well-formed, trench. Over his right shoulder on the parapet is a mystery device with a bolt action similar to a rifle. It possibly might have been used for sending off signal flares or grenades.

Three members of Infantry Regiment Nr. 148 pose in a rather drab looking studio setting. The date on the reverse is January 17, 1915, and they are all seen wearing M1910 tunics. The NCO on the left is armed with a holstered pistol and a Prussian Infanterie Offiziers Degen IOD 89 with a portapee indicating his high status as an NCO.

This NCO proudly grips his Saxon model IOD 89 sword as he sits for his portrait wearing his M1910 tunic and crusher visor cap. The shoulder boards of his tunic bear the cypher of the Saxon Leib Grenadier Regiment Nr. 100.

Two swordsmen wearing the M1895 uniform cross their weapons in a mock duel. The blade on the right carries a blued panel engraving depicting men on horseback and appears to be an artillery model.

BELOW: A most interesting documentary photograph of the promotion ceremony of an NCO of the Bavarian Infantry Regiment Nr. 3. He has been promoted to senior NCO status as indicated by the engraved blade sword held by the third man from the left, the portapee held by the next man and the sword belt and hangers held by the next. Flowers, two bottles of Cabinet champagne, and ten glasses lend a festive air to the occasion. An interesting mixture of uniforms and helmets are seen, a Litewka, an M1895 and M1910 tunic, three ersatz brass-trimmed pickelhaube, three brass-trimmed M1895 pickelhaube and an officer's grade helmet on the Offizierstellvertrater making the award.

This training photograph of Bavarian troops was mailed 17 December 1914. Close inspection reveals many interesting details. The two well-padded recruits lower left and right are dressed for bayonet training, a rifle target is raised in the center background, a man in the rear row holds up his hobnailed boots, the Sergeant Major stands sword in hand with his other NCOs in the foreground, and all the recruits are in M1895 training uniforms.

An unusual study of an infantry NCO mounted on a handsome dappled gray horse. On the reverse the subject dedicated the picture to his friends and comrades of the 1914-1917 war and is dated 1 July 1917. He is carrying a gas mask and is armed with a stag-handled trench fighting knife indicating he was not too far from the front.

Uniforms and Equipment of the Imperial German Army 1900-1918

Ersatz bayonets at the ready and beer to be consumed are two activities seen in this photograph of Württemberg Infantry Regiment Nr. 126 during the training process. The man seated far left may have something added to his beer if the barber is not careful how he cuts his hair.

Seven Bavarians in M1910 uniforms, one of whom has been awarded the Iron Cross 2nd Class, pose with fixed bayonets somewhere in France on 28 March 1915. They are armed with Gew. 98.s and with S98 bayonets. The bayonet on the rifle second from the left appears to have a wider blade and may be an example of the saw-back version.

A Bavarian NCO in an outdoor winter pose. He wears an M1910 tunic and displays the NCO tresse on his collar and cuffs. The extra Bavarian blue and white borte tape edge his collar and a Bavarian brass-trimmed pickelhaube and belt buckle complete this identification. He is carrying a ribbed-handled trench fighting knife with a bayonet knot, or troddel, indicating his role as a front-line soldier.

Two visor-capped infantrymen pose for an anonymous photographer, and of interest, is the stag-handled trench fighting knife and open-claw belt worn by the NCO on the right. He also wears Garde litzen on the M1915 bluse and a Schützen Abzeichen for marksmanship proficiency.

Uniforms and Equipment of the Imperial German Army 1900-1918

The large stag grip on his trench fighting knife cost this NCO extra marks when he selected this private purchase weapon. He wears with his knife an open-clawed buckled belt, a salty crusher visor cap, cavalry trousers reinforced with leather, and well-polished laced boots and leather gaiters. The reverse identifies the subject at George Haage and is dated 1916.

Uniforms and Equipment of the Imperial German Army 1900-1918

A rarity is shown here: an unusual model S15 bayonet with its one piece grip is fixed on this infantryman's Gew 98. The reverse of the photograph is dated November 1916, in Russia. Also of note are the glasses worn by our subject which are those issued to be worn under the gas mask, although there is no evidence of a gas mask in the picture.

This freshly equipped young infantryman is in full marching gear, an M1910/15 uniform, and a Gew 98. fixed with an unusual ersatz bayonet with a pressed steel hilt. By his left foot is the photograph identity block numbered 2296 which he used to redeem his picture from the Otto Dubielzig Studio located in the Munster-lager.

Uniforms and Equipment of the Imperial German Army 1900-1918

One would assume this photograph was taken near the front. The water-filled shell hole looks like it's not recent, but the Gummimask gas mask is at the ready; the presence of the gas mask glasses and the trench fighting knife show that danger is not far away.

M1895 Blue Uniform

Trainees during wartime were issued M1895 uniforms to save wear and tear on the M1910, 1910/15 and M1915 uniforms to be used later in the field. This Bavarian infantryman was photographed by Oscar Hepperlin, one of the professional studio operators at the Hammelburg training area. Our subject wears a Bavarian brass-trimmed M1895 pickelhaube, M1889 patronentaschen, or cartridge boxes, M1895 tornister, or field pack, Stiefel M1901 marching boots, M1909 Spaten, or entrenching tool, and is armed with a Gew 98. and a S98/05 bayonet.

Uniforms and Equipment of the Imperial German Army 1900-1918

Three Württemberg recruits pose for A. Bässler, the photographer in Münsingen, wearing their training M1895 uniforms, brass-trimmed M1895 pickelhauben with Württemberg frontplates and newly issued brown Stiefel marching boots of the M1901 pattern. They are equipped with M1895 patronentaschen cartridge boxes, M1895 packs, and Gew 98.s with S98 bayonets.

This photograph of trainees of Ersatz Reserve Infantry Regiment 149 shows graphically the vast differences in age of those involved in the creation of the new wartime army. Teenagers and men in their forties are shown wearing a mixture of M1895 and cotton drill uniforms. Footwear varies from carpet slippers to M1893 schnürschuh side-laced shoes to M1901 marching boots. Two men armed with Gew 98.s wear brass-trimmed M1895 pickelhauben with reserve crosses affixed to the frontplates. The wear and tear given to these old uniforms is evidenced by the large patch on the left chest of the next to last man on the right back row.

This group photograph of the 8. Korporalschaft of the Saxon Reserve Infantry Regiment 107 was taken for their farewell to training. The card was mailed from Leipzig on 28 April 1915 showing them all wearing the M1895 uniforms, mützen, or caps, and two with brass-trimmed M1895 pickelhauben with Saxon frontplates. Of interest is the small red white and black patriotic banner displayed over the identification sign. The condition of the uniforms seems to be better than those seen in the previous photograph.

A wartime recruit in the 2nd Garde Grenadier Regiment stands dressed for sentry duty in his M1895 tunic with its Garde litzen clearly shown. The crown and cypher on the shoulder straps identify him as a 2nd Garde Grenadier and the Garde eagle on his pickelhaube confirms that status. The patronentaschen cartridge boxes are M1895 and his weapon is a Gew 98.

The date was 3 December 1913 when this photograph of three Bavarian recruits from Bavarian Infantry Regiment 11 was mailed from the Deggendorf Kasern near Gratenwohr. The happy faces shown in this exceptionally clear picture must reflect their peace time status and the fine condition of their equipment. The chinstrap on the lower right helmet appears to be of the earlier 1887 style and all uniforms, and other equipment are M1895.

A recruit from the Württemberg Grenadier Regiment Nr. 123 poses for his studio portrait wearing his M1895 tunic with Grenadier litzen and the regimental crown and cypher shoulder straps. He is wearing laced shoes and an M1895 brass-trimmed pickelhaube with the Württemberg frontplate. An M1895 tornister pack, M1909 patronentaschen cartridge boxes, Gew 98. rifle and S98 bayonet round out his equipment.

Württemberg Infantry Regiment Nr. 180 was the home for these three early war recruits in September of 1914. The M1895 uniforms are evident and the musician wears the Schwalbennester, or swallow's nest, shoulder insignia. He also carries a bugle, and a fife case is on his belt. Two men are wearing newly issued brown marching boots while the man in the center is wearing the M1893 side laced schnürschuh. M1895 pickelhauben carry the Württemberg frontplate and the rifle is a Gew 98. with an S98 bayonet. The card is postmarked Tübingen.

The helmet frontplate identifies this soldier as being from a Baden regiment. The M1895 blue uniform he is wearing seems to have a collar many times larger than necessary, which is an indication of training issue. He is carrying dress white gloves and wears a patent leather dress belt.

A fine portrait of a Württemberg reserve officer candidate taken by the Vollmar Studio in Stuttgart. His M1907 gray mantel, or overcoat, bears the candy-striped edge shoulder straps of a one-year volunteer and is open to show his M1895 blue tunic. A handsome officer's grade pickelhaube with the Württemberg arms frontplate completes his costume.

From the elite Garde Regiment zu Fuss, this young recruit has chosen a pickelhaube with the Garde Eagle frontplate, parade Haarbush, M1907 Mantel, and M1895 uniform as the dress for his formal portrait. He is wearing M1901 front-laced schnürschuh, but if we look at the wrinkles at his cuff, marching boots had recently been worn.

Uniforms and Equipment of the Imperial German Army 1900-1918

A pre-war photograph of four members of the Hessian Infantry Regiment Nr. 118. On their M1895 tunics, IR 118 wore white shoulder boards with a crown and cypher, plus white patches on their cuffs. The distinctive Hessian belt plates and helmet frontplates can be seen in this picture.

An einjahrig-freiwillige, or one-year volunteer, from Baden Infantry Regiment 111. He wears the NCO buttons on his collar and one-year volunteer yellow and red striping on the shoulder straps of his M1895 tunic. The detail of the Baden Griffin helmet plate shows up well in this photograph.

A young recruit from the Württemberg Grenadier Regiment 119 poses in an outdoor setting wearing his guard duty uniforms. The M1895 tunic bears Grenadier litzen and the Württemberg frontplate shows up well on his M1895 pickelhaube. He is armed with a Gew 98. and a S98/05a bayonet.

Minenwerfer (Mortars) and Crews

A mortarman makes a fine adjustment on a Leichte Minenwerfer neuer/Art. or new model light mortar. It was of 76 mm caliber with a range of 1200-1400 yards depending on the type of shell. This piece was also known as the "Ehrhardt" minenwerfer.

A picture worthy of close study taken at the Minenwerferschule der 4 Armee Belgien. Here we see the Leichte Minenwerfer n.A with its crew and accessories. The mortar itself is on its base with wheels on either side for mobility. The two long bars crossed in front are the transport handles which are inserted into the lugs on the edge of the base. The man kneeling on the left holds the bore cleaning brush while the box on the right holds tools and small accessories. The crew being trained are Landsturmers from the XVIII Army Corps District, 2nd Batallion as shown by their collar devices. The two NCOs are equipped with Fernglas 08 binoculars. The man on the far left is wearing an M15 Bluse which would date the photo no earlier than 1916.

Another Leichte Minenwerfer n.A in a trench firing position. The crew all wear the M15 field bluse and most have gas masks slung in readiness. The man in the foreground holds the firing lanyard, the man to his left is the loader, the man on the far left the aimer, and on the far right is the communications man on the field phone in touch with the forward observers.

A crew from Füsilier Regiment Nr. 73 with a Leichte Minenwerfer n.A loading a shell prior to firing from a concealed position. The crew are wearing the M15 field bluse and mützen.

A Leichte Minenwerfer n.A. in the transporting mode as can be seen by the two long bars protruding toward the rear and the spares box mounted behind the gun. A shell in the foreground gives some perspective as to its size. The crew are wearing M1910/15 uniforms.

A formal portrait of a decorated Prussian Minenwerfer Unteroffizier wearing an M1915 Feldbluse. The shoulder straps are black with red piping and "MW" chainstitched in red which is difficult to see without a magnifying glass.

A permanent trench firing position is the location of this Leichte Minenwerfer n.A. Close inspection of the photograph shows the ranging table and nomenclature on the base plate just in front of the 76 mm projectile.

On June 31, 1917 this crew wearing cotton drill jackets were photographed with a Leichte Minenwerfer n.A. From the photo one can see the transport wheels removed and located on the ground on either side of the aimer; one of the axles is right in front of his foot. The evidence of gas mask straps and containers indicates a proximity to the front.

Small but deadly is the best description of this Leichte Minenwerfer n.A. in a trench firing position. All metal transport wheels, different than the standard, are leaning against the wall in the background.

The Minenwerfer takes on a new role as a direct fire anti-tank weapon. Notice the modified frame which gives the gun a straight field of fire and the artillery wheeled transport carriage.

Another view of the same piece showing greater detail of the heavy steel firing frame, as well as the carriage.

By August 1918 when this photograph was taken, the Leichte Minenwerfer n.A. had gone through many changes of basic usages. This photograph shows how a mortar can become a field piece. The trail frame has been enlarged and the addition of a trail stabilizer has made the transition a reality. The dismountable wheels allow the mortar to become a fixed weapon.

A seven-man crew poses by their Leichte Minenwerfer n.A. with the direct fire trail Carriage near Verdun, 27 May 1918. Each man seen demonstrates his function in the crew. Loaders, fuse setters, gun layers, lanyard firing operator, and NCO all have a job to do. Four of the seven have been awarded the Iron Cross 2nd Class, so this is a combat group.

May 28, 1917 finds these Leichte Minenwerfer n.A. crews on the Eastern front. The crews wear a mixture of M1910 and M1915 Feldbluse uniforms with many ribbons for the Iron Cross 2nd Class in evidence. The mortars are in their original configuration with their long trails showing at both lower extremes of the photograph.

A ten-man crew tends to this Leichte Minenwerfer n.A. somewhere in France. A mixture of M1910/15 and M1915 uniforms dates the photograph into 1916 at least. Iron Cross 2nd Class ribbons are worn by several members of this crew indicating that their presence at the front has been for some period of time.

Six men form a crew for a Granatenwerfer Model F, 1916. The purpose of this grenade launcher was to throw a grenade from a fixed position a minimum of 55 yards to a maximum of 328 yards. As can be seen, the projectile or grenade is placed over a projection rod. The propelling charge is fitted in the projectile and when discharged, fires the grenade. The weight of the grenade is between 4 to 5 1/2 pounds.

Members of Infantry Regiment Nr. 24 pose with a Granatenwerfer Model F, 1916. This photograph shows how small and simple this weapon was. The man on the right holds the firing lanyard. M1910, M1910/15 and M1915 uniforms are worn by this crew.

July 7, 1917 found this group of trainees from Ersatz Batallion Nr. 14 training in the use of grenades. The Grenatenwerfer Model F, 1916 is in the center of the photograph, while many of the group are holding various models of the stick grenade. All but two in the photo are wearing M1895 training tunics with white drill trousers.

An infantry Feldwebel-Leutnant, which is a rare rank, demonstrates a Grenatenwerfer Model F, 1916. He holds the grenade prior to fixing it to the projection rod. The date is July 1916.

Troops from Minenwerfer Abteilung 18 take a summer break in front of a church in Russia. Four Leichte Minenwerfer n.A. can be seen on the left and stacked Gew 98.s on the right. The colt held by the NCO on the left may be spoils of war.

BELOW: An unshaven Bavarian wearing an M1910 uniform poses with a variety of unexploded French mortar rounds, a rifle grenade, and a German 170 mm Minenwerfer round standing over its wicker protective basket.

A close-up photograph of a Mittlere (Medium) Minenwerfer alter Art. 170 mm. The optic sight can be seen on the upper right, as well as the tip of a projectile protruding from the muzzle.

Another view of the medium mortar old model, Mittlere Minenwerfer (170 mm) alter Art. in its firing position in a trench location, with the optic sight in place. Wicker shell carriers and a Gew 98. can be seen in the background.

A Mittlere Minenwerfer as seen from the rear in its wheeled transport configuration. The muzzle cover is in position and close examination of the photo shows picks, shovels and other tools in their allocated locations. The reverse of the card is dated 26 August 1918.

A frontal view of the Mittlere Minenwerfer 170 mm resting on a railroad flatcar. Another mortar is on the next flatcar and a variety of other field artillery pieces are seen in the background. What appears to be a bullet or shrapnel scar is on the near wheel at ten o'clock.

A five-man crew and their Mittlere Minenwerfer (170 mm) alter Art. with all accessories. This weapon in action weighed 1,232 pounds and could throw a gas or incendiary shell 1,300 yards, or high explosive shell, which was heavier, 1000 yards. Of particular interest in this photo is the man on the far right who was the loader and barrel swabber who wore a special arm and shoulder covering to protect his uniform from grease and burnt powder residue. A mixture of M1910, M1910/15 and M1915 uniforms are worn by this crew from Minenwerfer Batallion IV. The reverse is dated 12 September 1916 at Feld-Poststation 409.

Another view and crew of a 170 mm Mittlere Minenwerfer which is in the mobile configuration with the wheels and towing bar in place. The awesome dimensions of the projectile are clearly evident in this photograph.

Is there a minenwerfer cavalry? Ten "riders" are astride ten 170 mm minenwerfers as part of a gala party as evidenced by the wine bottles and glasses on the table in the foreground. Spring was the season, but the place and year are unknown.

A Mittlere Minenwerfer alter Art. in the transport mode near its firing position. Note the large pile of empty wicker shell baskets, and in the far background, a crew is moving a mortar on its wheels.

An example of the smoothbore "Lanz" 91 mm Minenwerfer. Not a great deal is known about these types of which Mauser built an almost identical model.

The crew surrounding this medium Minenwerfer seems to be studying it intently. Its canister-type projectile stands beside it on the dirt floor of a bunker. Close inspection of the base discloses no axle stubs for the mounting of wheels; instead there are lifting handles on either side where the tube attaches.

A sunlit crew in the M1915 bluse and shirtsleeves prepare to fire a Medium Minenwerfer. The projectile is in the tube and the firing lanyard can be seen by the hand of the man on the left.

The French Musée de L'Armée (Army Museum) produced postcards during the war and the money from their sale benefited wartime charities. The charity to help military wounded was the recipient of the sale of this card showing three different captured minenwerfer: a Mittlere Minenwerfer a. A., a 180 cm smooth bore and a Mittlere Minenwerfer n.A. The card states these were captured on the Champagne Front in 1915.

Stahlhelm - Steel Helmets

A Kanonier from the Württemberg Field Artillery Regiment 65 poses for a front-line photograph wearing an M1915 Feldbluse and an M1916 Stahlhelm. An interesting detail are the special ersatz shoulder straps issued in 1915.

A nice close-up of a Gefreiter of the Bavarian Infantry Regiment Nr. 4 wearing an M1910/15 tunic and an M1916 Stahlhelm. He has been awarded two Bavarian bravery awards, but no Iron Cross as yet. He is armed with a Kar 98a as seen slung on his back. The reverse is dated 20 December 1916 on the Somme.

Unteroffizier M. Christer of Pionier Kompanie 404 posed for this photograph on 3 July 1917 wearing his M1915 Feldbluse, marksmanship lanyard, M1895 patronentaschen ammunition pouches, leg-wraps, schnürschuh 1901 front-laced shoes, and the ribbon for the Iron cross 2nd Class. An M1916 Stahlhelm and a Gew 98. put him in readiness for action.

The photographer takes us into the trenches with this nice view of four members of Grenadier Regiment Nr. 4. They are wearing M1916 Stahlhelm and a combination of M1910 and M1915 tunics. Collar and cuff litzen are in evidence, as are three ribbons for the Iron Cross 2nd Class. Gew 98.s, a Kar 98a, and M1915 Gummimaske gas masks are in readiness at this front-line location. The card was mailed on 16 November 1917 by Unteroffizier Pfeiffer of Grenad. Rgt. No. 4. 12th Komp.

Uniforms and Equipment of the Imperial German Army 1900-1918

A Bavarian Gefreiter from Bavarian Infantry Regiment Nr. 4 sent this card on 23 January 1918 to a friend in Feld-Art. Rgt. 2, 9. Batallion. He is equipped with an M1916 Stahlhelm, a Kar 98a, a gas mask in its metal can, a Feldflasche 1893 canteen, and a brotbeutel 1887 breadbag attached to his belt.

An infantryman in combat order poses somewhere in France for this field portrait. An M1916 Stahlhelm, a Ledermaske (leather mask) gas mask, M1910 tunic, M1909 patronentaschen cartridge boxes, and a Gew 98. make up his equipment.

Ten Pioniers in assault equipment, M1916 Stahlhelm, M1910 and M1915 uniforms, M1895 patronentaschen cartridge boxes and Gew 98.s pose in the ruins of a French village.

June 2, 1917 was the date this card was mailed by the Feldpost of the 6th Company of Reserve Infantry Regiment 260 from Toulie, France. The group in the foreground are equipped with assault packs, grenade bags, M1916 Stahlhelm and Gew 98.s. It is interesting to note they all wear plain slip-on covers over the numbers on their shoulder straps. In the background visor caps, pickelhauben and various models of uniforms can be seen.

Heinrich Kittmann of Reserve Infantry Regiment Nr. 110 mailed this photograph of himself to a friend on 7 July 1917. At the time he was part of the 4. Kompanie on the Western front and posed in an M1910 uniform, M1916 Stahlhelm, M1909 patronentaschen ammunition boxes and a Gew 98.

BELOW: An interesting photograph of "the Ladies From Hell", as the Scottish-kilted regiments were known, as prisoners carrying German wounded to the rear. Their guards are wearing a combination of mützen caps and M1916 Stahlhelm. The date was May 1918.

This card picturing six members of Infantry Regiment 84 was mailed to a Saxon family on 8 June 1917. All are wearing the M1907 field gray overcoats, one of which has been shortened approximately 6 inches. The soldiers would fashion leg-wraps from this cut off material until orders prohibited shortening the coats. Three of the M1916 Stahlhelms show the early gloss paint, while the one in the center is of a duller finish. Two men are still wearing the M1915 pickelhauben, covered, and minus the spikes.

A combination of M1916 Stahlhelm and M1915 pickelhauben helmets were being worn in this group photograph of Minenwerfer Kompagnie 309. All but a few are wearing M1910 and 1910/15 tunics, many are equipped with gas masks in the canvas carriers and the majority are in full marching gear.

Five members of an artillery battery pose in mixed uniform. The man armed with a Kar 98a and with an M1916 helmet wears an M1910/15 tunic and cotton drill trousers, the next three wearing mützen with the black artillery band are in M1915 blusen and the fifth wears a cotton drill work jacket and feldgrau wool trousers. So much for "the uniform of the day" regulation. The reverse is dated 10 July 1910.

A rather strange photograph of unusual weapons and accessories. A T-Gewehr anti-tank rifle made by Mauser in 13 mm missing its bi-pod rests on an M1916 Stahlhelm with the armored frontal plate, and on the two stools rests a 20 mm prototype model automatic cannon made in 1918 at the Rheinmetall plant at Dusseldorf. It was invented by the director, Heinrich Ehrhardt, who was world famous for his developments in field artillery.

Uniforms and Equipment of the Imperial German Army 1900-1918

Decorative Steins, Pipes and Patriotic Items

The Naval base at Kiel was the location of the studio which took this photograph of four sailors from the reserve ship *S.M.S. Pelikan*. There are three steins and a flask in this view all with Naval motifs. The lids on the steins have finials in the form of standing sailors and the flask is decorated with a ship's wheel and Imperial crown motifs. All four men are carrying souvenir walking sticks with ribbons or tallies attached. The reverse is dated 28 February 1911. The *Pelikan* was a mine layer, completed in 1891; in 1914 it served on coastal defense, and by 1917 was a training and experimental ship.

Dressed in M1895 uniforms, two NCOs and two recruits pose with a variety of steins for Metz photographer, H. Eberhard. One on the left bears a train motif, next bears the portrait of King Ludwig of Bavaria, and the last two feature the Kaiser. The legends around the top edges of the steins are all different and they all lack the traditional style domed lids.

Litewka tunics and M1895 uniforms are the uniforms of preference for these six men of Bavarian Infantry Regiment Nr. 15 in this 1914 photograph. The mixture of size and styles of their steins may vary with their individual capacities, and it is interesting to note that none of them bear military decorations.

A group of recruits from Bavarian Infantry Regiment 16 pose with their NCOs in the garrison at Passau. The recruits are all wearing M1895 tunics and corduroy trousers. The stein in the center is a tall reservist style with a pewter lid surmounted with a miniature infantryman offering a toast. "The right thumb in the tunic pose" seems to be popular among the recruits in this photograph. The mailing date of the card was 14 January 1917.

A humorous pose is taken by reservists of the 10th Kompagnie 4. Bavarian Infantry Regiment at Metz in 1913. Every man in the group carries his decorated flask on a striped cord over his shoulder and most carry various styles of decorated canes, both items prized by members of the reserve. All are photographed dressed in M1895 uniforms and the studio artist has outdone himself with the painting of the auto, as well as the backdrop of Metz with airships and airplanes overhead.

The war must have seemed a long way off to this well-fed Bavarian wearing an M1910/15 tunic, corduroy trousers and slippers sitting next to a garden. He sits with a large civilian stein and a patriotic porcelain pipe with crossed flags. The reverse indicates the location was Garmisch and the date 8 August 1916.

Two Kanonier, cigars in hand, wearing cotton drill work uniforms pose with their steins topped with artillery shell lids. The postmark on the reverse is dated 12 May 1905 and sent from the town of Grebach.

Outdoor drinking and smoking by these three Bavarians, on what appears to be the Vogesen Mountain front, was somewhat limited by the lack of glasses and matches. Close inspection of the label of the left hand bottle indicates the contents to be "Citronensyrup", or lemonade, while the other may have been a cherry flavored drink. They are wearing M1910/15 uniforms in this undated photograph.

Six Bavarians take a lunch break during field maneuvers. With steins, bottles, bread and mess tins, they are pictured in front of a fire pit which is emitting a small amount of smoke. They wear a variety of work uniforms and the M1893 side-lacing schnürschuh boots.

Uniforms and Equipment of the Imperial German Army 1900-1918

An unusual view of the Bavarian Fuss Artillerie Regiment Nr. 2 wearing fresh M1910 tunics with M1895 mounted troops trousers, tall cavalry boots and dark blue mützen (caps) with black bands. One glass and two stoneware steins of civilian design are proudly displayed as well as many cigars in this photograph taken 7 December 1914.

Prussian Eagle flags, streamers and a large green and white Saxon flag replace patriotic steins and flasks in this photograph of four recently trained recruits from Saxon Infantry Regiment 139. They are all dressed in newly issued M1910 uniforms, M1909 patronentaschen pouches, M1895 tornister field packs, M1895 pickelhaube helmets with field covers and are armed with Gew 98. rifles with S98 bayonets. The reverse is dated 11 December 1914.

100

Three soldiers wearing cotton drill fatigue uniforms pose astride a beer keg for an informal portrait. Two hold ornate non-lidded civilian steins, while the man in the center cradles what appears to be a bottle of Champagne in his left arm. They are wearing the M1906 side-seamed hobnailed marching boots, or stiefel. Unit identification is not possible.

Two friends and members of Bavarian Infantry Regiment 15 pose for an informal photograph. The man on the left is wearing an M1895 uniform and is holding a civilian stein with heavy decoration and a pewter lid. His friend wears a cotton drill work jacket and his mütze at a rakish angle. The reverse is dated 5 February 1911 and was mailed from Neuburg am Donau.

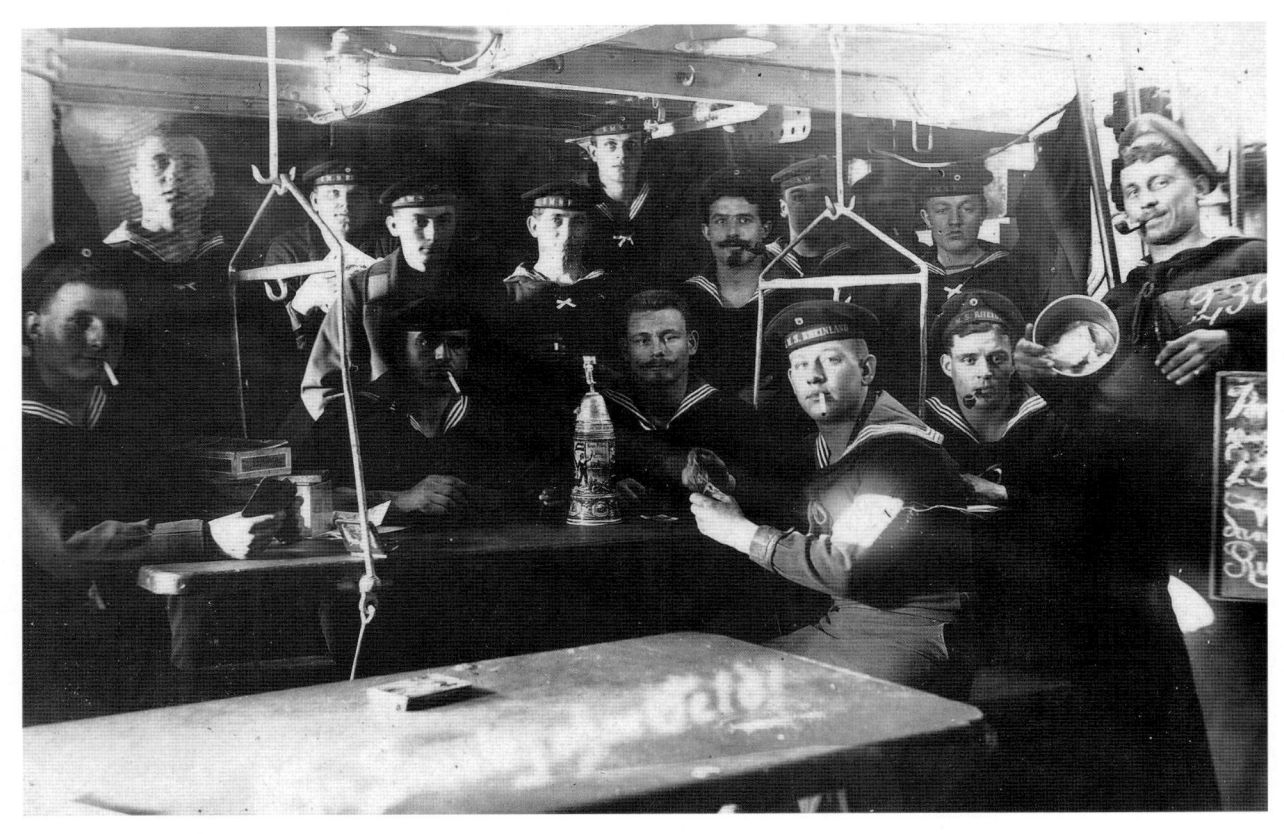

Below decks aboard the *S.M.S. Rheinland*, the crew are at leisure. A great example of a Naval decorated stein is on the table between the card players, while pipes and cigarettes are enjoyed by many of the group. The *S.M.S. Rheinland* was a Westfalen Class battleship launched in September of 1908, and was scrapped at Dordrecht in 1922. She was present at the Battle of Jutland and was damaged by stranding in the Baltic in April of 1918.

This photograph was taken by the studio of L. Führer in Munich 1917. The men all appear to be recruits with the exception of the stern NCO who was guiding them through the training process. Five plain stoneware steins are displayed, as well as a beer keg in the center. The two sentries on each end of the picture wear M1910 tunics with later models of the tornister pack with webbing straps, while the others are equipped with M1910/15 uniforms.

Five out of the six men in this group are wearing the ribbon of the Iron Cross 2nd Class; one actually wears the medal and a marksman's lanyard, as they relax by their dugout quaintly named "Villa-Liesel". Beer either from the bottle, glass, or glass stein seemed to be plentiful for this well-fed and happy group from Infantry Regiment Nr. 110. M1910 uniforms and walking sticks were the fashion of the day. Of interest is the offiziers' sponton visible between the two men in the left rear.

Outdoor beer drinking was a popular pastime when the enemy shells were not falling as this photograph proves. Members of Feld-Artillerie Regiments 20 and 30, as well as Reserve FAR 11, don't look overly happy at this moment in history and some of the glass steins are empty, possibly the reason for the glum looks.

Three members of the Dockyard Division at the Naval base at Kiel posed for this wonderfully clear portrait by Carl Dreyer of Kiel. The tall steins with profuse Naval decorations have ornate pewter lids topped with cast figures of sailors holding flags. The reverse bears the date of 3 December 1916.

Two infantrymen from Bavarian Infantry Regiment 10 pose for their portrait at the Wendsche Studio in Ingolstadt. Supplied with two large reservist steins with Bavarian lion thumbpieces on their pewter tops and in M1895 uniforms, they are well set for this occasion.

This young Pionier has finished his training and is preparing to leave for the front. His M1915 pickelhaube, without spike, is topped with green leaves and a bouquet. A patriotic flag depicting Kaiser Wilhelm is placed next to his Gew 98. with attached S98/05 bayonet.

Four medics seated in a hospital railcar are enjoying their pipes. The near man on the left has a large porcelain reservist pipe, while the others are more plainly equipped. The visor caps are of the style issued to medical troops and the tunics are M1910 issue. The reverse is dated France, 10 March 1916.

Christmas-time in a billet somewhere in France is being celebrated in a number of ways by these members of Bavarian Infantry Regiment Nr. 2. Reading, playing three-handed Skat, eating and smoking pipes and cigars are all popular. A small decorated tree can be seen in the background.

No steins are evident in this picture, but there seems to be an ample amount of beer, forty bottles in all. The First Sergeant, or Speis, is standing in the center of this group who appear to be awaiting lunch on a balmy summer day. The view was taken by W. Meyer from Esslingen, but the date is unknown.

This happy Bavarian NCO is enjoying an afternoon off duty. On the table before him he has his plain briar pipe, his stoneware one-liter stein from a Munich brewery, a loaf of bread, and an empty Feldpost mailing carton.

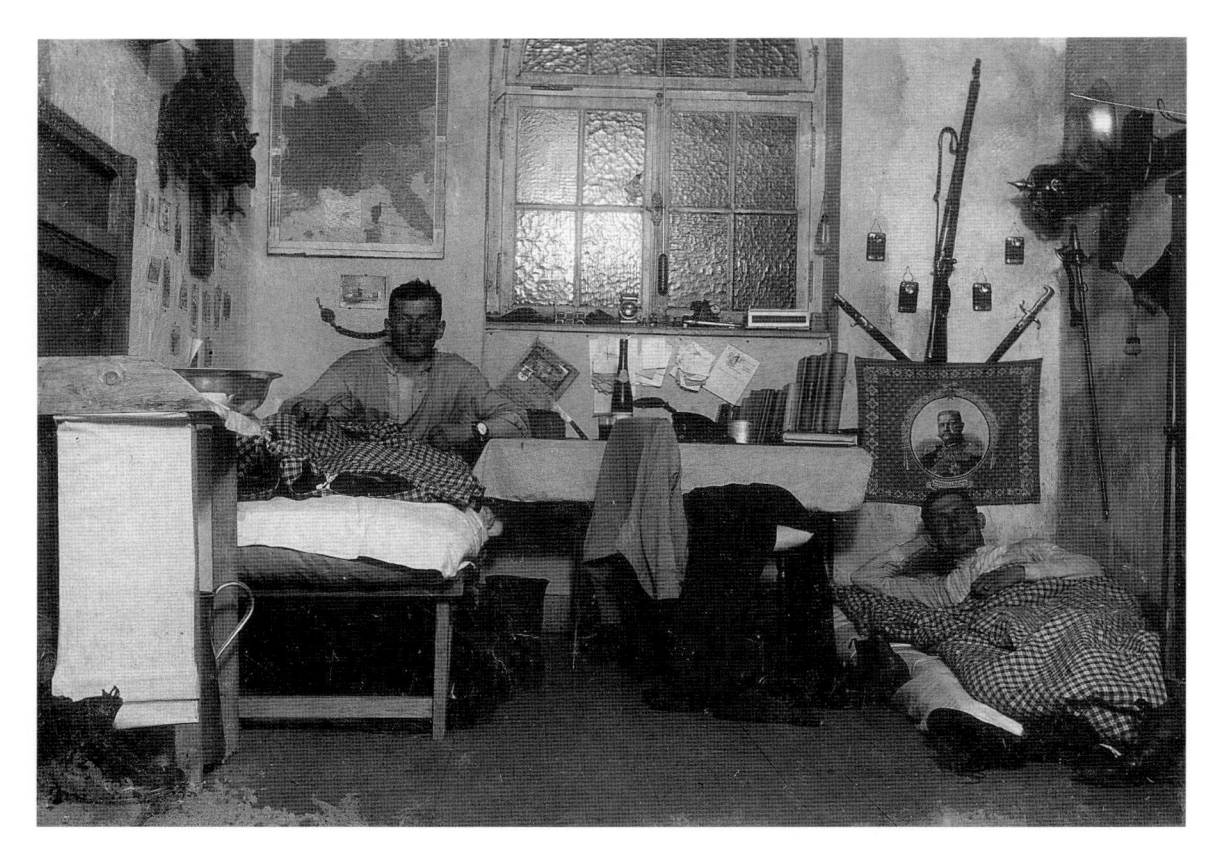

Not an exciting view, but one of interest, as it is one seldom seen in photographs. This is the interior of a sleeping area of the 2. Ersatz Batallion of Baden Infantry Regiment 112 somewhere in France. On the wall are four flashlights, a Kar 98a, S98 and S71 bayonets, a printed cloth picture of General Hindenberg, a sword, a pickelhaube, a marksmanship lanyard, and a situation map of the campaigns in Europe. A long-necked bottle of wine, a partially filled glass, as well as a group of books are on the table between the two soldiers' bunks. The reverse is marked to the 2. ERS. Btl. I.R.112, but with no date.

The recruits of Stube 119 pose in a variety of uniforms, performing a variety of leisure activities. The date of this photograph is unknown, but in all probability was prior to the outbreak of hostilities. The uniforms include Litewkas, M1895 tunics, shirtsleeves, cotton drill fatigue jackets, visor caps, mützen and pickelhauben. This dress mix and the various leisure activities was certainly portrayed by design of the photographer.

Life in the Württemberg reserves, Room 92 was well-portrayed in this photograph by Alfred Hirrlinger of Stuttgart. Smoking from fancy reservists pipes, beer drinking from stoneware steins, accordion playing, bathing, record keeping, cleaning, and shaving were the many recorded activities of these Württembergers. The sign on the lower left tells one and all there are 280 days to serve. This is a pre-war photo and of interest are the litewkas worn by the two men in visor caps in the center.

A decorated Dragoon on the left in his M1910 uniform is in charge of dispensing spirits, sausages and smokes to an eager group of clients. He has a variety of available drinks, and a full box of cigars on the rear of his sutler's wagon. The large dog in the foreground shows little or no concern, and the variety of uniforms and pipes is certainly a broad one.

Telegraph and Signal Troops

The soldier on the far left holds a hand-held blinker signal light, as does the man on the far right. Next to them are the men responsible for receiving the return messages and next to them are the message readers with Fernglas 08 binoculars. The signalers proficiency patch can be seen on the sleeve of the signaler on the left. They are armed with Gew 98.s.

A group of Signal trainees of Infantry Regiment 58 pose with their instructors in front of one of the regimental buildings. The electrical blinker signal devices, the message recorders and the training NCOs, one wearing a silver wound badge, are prominent in the photograph. Model 1915 service blouses and a few M1910/15 tunics are being worn by these troops.

A signaler from Infantry Regiment Nr. 57 carries a round battery operated blinker signal device on his belt. He is wearing an M1910/15 uniform, a covered M1915 pickelhaube, and is carrying M1909 patronentaschen ammo pouches and a Kar 98a.

BELOW: Telegraph troops wearing their shakos, black-trimmed M1895 tunics and cotton drill work trousers pose by a garden while on maneuvers. They are equipped with field phones, bicycles, and Kar 98a carbines. The senior NCO leaning on the rail in the center wears his marksmanship lanyard and medals from the 1870 war, and the third man from the right wears the candy-striped edging of a one-year volunteer on his shoulder straps.

A telegraph soldier and his family pose for the Dürr studio in Dieringhausen. He is wears an M1910 uniform and a brass telegraphers belt buckle which was longer than the standard buckle and had two attaching points for the telegraph wire reel when laying the line.

One sailor, third from the left amid a group of Kraftfahers, or motordrivers, and other Army types are photographed by two of their trucks in a village square. Two of the drivers are seen with two different versions of the round battery operated blinker signaling devices. The two drivers with the blinkers are armed with P. 08 Luger pistols and one wears a top hat with goggles.

Field Artillery Personnel

A photograph of a Kanonier from the mounted Feld-Artillerie Regiment Nr. 2 in a formal pose with his wife, dated 7 October 1914. He is wears an M1895 artillery tunic with black collar and cuffs with white shoulder straps with a red flaming grenade and the number "2". His ball-topped pickelhaube bears the special frontplate with "F.R." in a circular plate on the eagle's chest which was unique to Feld-Artillerie regiments 1, 2, 3, and 6. He wears tall mounted troops boots and carries an M1874 Artillery model sword.

A munitions column driver from the machine gun company of Infantry Regiment 121 poses for his portrait in August of 1915. He wears a field-covered M1915 ball-topped pickelhaube, an M1910 tunic, mounted-style stiefel-hose, or trousers, mounted-style boots, and a mounted-style open claw buckled belt. He is armed with an M1879/83 Armee-Revolver and an artillery model sword, M1874.

A photo of a similarly dressed Kanonier from Württemberg Feld-Artillerie Regiment Nr. 49, second battery, was attached to the 27th Infantry Division when this was taken 28 May 1915. Details of the pistoletasche, or holster, for the M1883 revolver and the M1874 artilleriesäbel, or sword, are clearly seen in this view.

Members of the 1st Garde Feld-Artillerie regiment are pictured in front of a monument which is marked "Paris" in this photograph taken by Atelier Günteritz, Berlin. The training NCOs are wearing their M1895 uniforms and the recently trained troops are wearing their freshly issued M1910 uniforms and covered M1915 ball-topped pickelhaube helmets. All have been issued Kar 88. carbines and M1874 artillery sabers, and as indicated by the flowers in evidence, are on their way to the front.

These members of Württemberg Fuss-Artillerie Regiment Nr. 13 have been recently equipped with new M1910 uniforms, M1907 Mantels, or overcoats, M1915 ball-topped pickelhauben with field covers, M1909 patronentaschen and M1895 tornister field packs. The issued weapons are Kar 98a carbines and S98/05 bayonets.

This studio portrait shows a mounted Kanonier from the Hessian Feld-Artillerie Regiment Nr. 25 wearing his M1895 parade uniform, visor cap, cavalry belt, mounted boots and Hessian dress sword. Note the litzen on his collar and cuffs worn only by Hessian FAR 25.

Uniforms and Equipment of the Imperial German Army 1900-1918

A Garde Feld-Artillerie NCO Kanonier is pictured prior to his departure for the front as indicated by the flowers by his Kar 98a carbine. He wears the M1910 uniform, ball-topped pickelhaube, and full marching equipment.

This Kanonier from Feld-Artillerie Regiment 42 is standing guard duty near his striped guard house at his home Kaserne, or barracks. Armed with a Kar 88. carbine, an S71 bayonet, single M1895 cartridge box and dressed in an M1910 tunic, cavalry-style boots and an M1915 pickelhaube without its ball-top, he typifies the uniform dress of 1916. The reverse of this photograph is dated 12 November 1916.

This photo postcard was mailed through the Feldpost of the XIX Armeekorps on 16 December 1915. The subject is an NCO with the Saxon Feld-Artillerie Regiment Nr. 78 who for protection against the cold, is wearing an M1909 mounted troops overcoat with NCO collar tabs and regimental shoulder straps. Saddlebags are slung over the horse in front of the rider, and the scabbard of his sword can be seen by his left foot.

A wonderful view of a Feld-Artillerie limber and ammunition wagon four-horse team. Each pair of horses has one rider, three men are sitting on the gun limber, or Feldprotze, and the three standing men would sit on the Muntionshinterwagen, or ammunition wagon, at the rear. All the troops are wearing M1916 Stahlhelm helmets, and M1910 and M1910/15 uniforms with a mixture of standard and cavalry-style belts.

Reserve Garde Fuss-Artillerie Kanoniers form a prone firing line. They are wearing M1910 uniforms, some with Brandenberg and some with Swedish cuffs, some with collar and cuff litzen, and some without. Their shoulder straps and ball-topped pickelhaube covers are without markings as per Garde Truppen regulations. They are armed with a mixture of Gew 98. and Kar 98a's, and the NCO kneeling at the end of the line is pointing his P. 08 Luger pistol at the camera. The long-style bugle with its cords wrapped tightly around the instrument is an interesting touch.

Four Kanoniers of the 12th Saxon Fuss-Artillerie Regiment pose for their photograph by an early Feldhaubitze with a solid trail. They wear M1910 uniforms, polished boots and ammunition pouches and are armed with Kar 98a carbines and S98/05 bayonets.

A well-armed group of Kanoniers from Baden Feld-Artillerie Regiment Nr. 66 sit for their portrait between two guardian lions at Garrison Lahr. The uniforms are M1910, the ball-topped pickelhauben M1895, some still with their rounded brass-scaled chinstraps, and the leather equipment shows a combination of various patronentaschen ammunition boxes and standard and cavalry-style belts. Weaponry consists of Gew 88. service rifles, Kar 98a carbines, M1883 Reichsrevolvers and artillery sabers M1874 known as Artilleriesäbel.

Smiles don't seem to be in order for the wedding photograph of this couple from Baden. The groom is an NCO with Baden Feld-Artillerie Regiment Nr. 76 from Freiburg. He is wears an M1915 Feldbluse with the ribbons for the Iron Cross 2nd Class and a Baden bravery decoration, and beside him sits an artillery model M1895 pickelhaube with a Baden frontplate and curved brass chinstrap scales.

A young Prussian Kanonier poses for his photograph celebrating the completion of his training. He is fully-equipped with all new gear including an M1915 Feldbluse, M1915 Artillery model pickelhaube with field cover, M1895 patronentaschen ammunition pouches, a Kar 98a with an S98/05 bayonet and an M1895 tornister field pack.

Another rather glum appearing couple pose for their wedding portrait at the Kleiber studio in Cannstatt. The serious Kanonier is serving with a Baden Artillery unit and is wearing an M1910 tunic with Brandenburg cuffs, riding breeches, cavalry-style boots, a mütze bearing the Baden cockade and carries an M1874 artillery saber.

Early in the war Hesse furnished two Feld-Artillerie Regiments, the 25th and the 61st. This Hessian Kanonier was assigned to the 25th and is seen wearing his new M1915 Feldbluse, mounted troops boots, M1895 patronentaschen on his belt with the Hessian buckle with a large crown. The ball-top has been removed from his pickelhaube and he is armed with a Kar 98a.

A Feld-Artillerie Kanonier wears his newly-issued M1910 uniform, side-seamed M1906 stiefel, or marching boots, a ball-topped pickelhaube and field cover for this end-of-training formal portrait. For a sidearm he was equipped with a KS 98 bayonet with a large troddel, or bayonet knot.

A Kanonier from Württemberg Feld-Artillerie Regiment 51, home on leave, poses with his wife and children for Gustav Scheerer, photographer in Esslingen. He wears an M1915 Feldbluse with the crown over "L" over a flaming bomb shoulder straps which were unique to FAR 51. The reverse is dated 5 May 1917.

Uniforms and Equipment of the Imperial German Army 1900-1918

The Carl Bauer Studio in Karlsruhe photographed this young member of Baden Feld-Artillerie Regiment 14 "Grossherzog", in February of 1917. His visor cap has been shaped to give it that special salty look and he wears an M1910 uniform, M1893 schnürschuh side-laced shoes, standard koppel, or belt, and is armed with the M1874 Artilleriesäbel, or sword. The crown over flaming bomb cypher of FAR 14 can be seen on his shoulder straps.

The flowers tell us that this Bavarian Feld-Artillerie Regiment 1 Kanonier was on his way to the front. He has been issued a feldgrau M1909 mounted troops overcoat, a pickelhaube with a spike rather than a ball as was regulation for the Bavarian artillery, tan M1909 patronentaschen cartridge boxes, and a Bavarian model brass lion's head short artillery sword. The cyphered shoulder straps of Bavarian FAR 1 are partially visible on his left shoulder. The photograph was taken by a Munich studio.

RIGHT: Dressed for Garrison guard duty, this Württemberg field artilleryman is in M1895 uniform, complete with an M1895 uncovered ball-topped pickelhaube with a Württemberg frontplate and convex scaled brass chinstrap, M1895 patronentaschen and is armed with a Kar 98a.

Uniforms and Equipment of the Imperial German Army 1900-1918

A French village street was the location for this photograph of a mounted Prussian Feld-Artillerie Kanonier. Interestingly, he is shown wearing his ball-topped M1895 pickelhaube with no field cover with his M1910 field artillery uniform. The M1874 Artilleriesäbel is carried in its saddle mount and details of the artillery horse furniture can be seen.

Many interesting details can be observed in this June 1915 photograph of members of 2. Garde Feld-Artillerie Regiment. They all wear the M1910 Garde uniforms with collar and cuff litzen, some with M1895 ball-topped pickelhauben, all with large red flaming bomb insignia on their shoulder straps designating 2. Garde FAR. Visible are an M1874 artillery saber, mounted troops boots by some, an M1883 revolver and holster, a dove-hilted artillery combat saber, 77 mm shells and their wicker carrying baskets. The reverse bears a Feldpost stamp for the 2. Garde Infanterie Division, and a cachet for 1. Abteilung 2. Garde Feld-Artillerie Regiment.

Uniforms and Equipment of the Imperial German Army 1900-1918

A team of horses and their rider from Württemberg Feld-Artillerie Regiment 65 are photographed on the Eastern front in Russia. This view gives a clear picture of the draft harness and tack necessary for pulling cannon and limbers. The Kanonier/driver wears a M1910 uniform, mounted troops boots, a covered M1915 ball-topped pickelhaube and is armed with an early M1879 Armeerevolver and a M1874 artillery saber.

These six one-year volunteers from Feld-Artillerie Regiment Nr. 11 were photographed near Cassel early in March 1914. The candy-striped einjahrig-freiwillege shoulder straps can be seen on their dark overcoats worn with dress white belts, as well as their M1895 brass-trimmed ball-topped pickelhauben with field covers and M1903 Fernglas binoculars.

Uniforms and Equipment of the Imperial German Army 1900-1918

Walking sticks are being displayed by these Kanoniers of Württemberg Feld-Artillerie Regiment 51 in this photograph taken somewhere in France. They are all wearing the M1910 uniforms, mounted troops boots, ball-topped pickelhauben with field covers marked with the regimental number 51. The pair in the front row are equipped with M1883 Reichsrevolvers carried on open buckle cavalry-style belts as is the man on the right rear. The FAR 51 crown, cypher L and flaming bomb identification can be seen on their shoulder straps.

BELOW: The Feldpost stamps on the reverse of this photocard indicate the subjects are from Landwehr Feld-Artillerie Regiment Nr. 4, 1. Abteilung, 2. Batterie and the date of mailing was 27 September 1917. They are dressed in a variety of M1910, M1910/15 and M1915 Feldbluse uniforms, some with cavalry-style boots, open buckle belts and mounted troops breeches and others with straight leg M1910 hose, or trousers.

128

Kraftfahrer Motordrivers and Vehicles

A Berlin studio named Kunstlichtatelier "Elektra" took this wonderful photo of a Prussian Kraftfahrer in his leather service uniform. The leather jacket, or lederrock, was initially designed in 1907 with modifications in 1912 and 1914. Originally they were of black leather and piped in red, with the collar insignia of an early automobile in brass; later in wartime, the leather was gray. Our subject is a Gefreiter and a reservist as indicated by the reserve cross on the cockade of his M1910 visored cap. Leather trousers, M1914 Ledergamasche neuerer Art gaiters and polished M1901 schnürshuh-laced boots complete his outfit. The lederrock buttons were silver-colored and the shoulder boards were red and black, later gray.

In warmer weather Kraftfahrer wore black cotton drill drivers uniforms, the same cut as the lederrock which is worn by these two drivers. The man in the rear seems to be posing rather than being an official passenger. The staff car was manufactured by Benz and carries the distinctive grille style used for many years. The reverse is dated 28 October 1915 by the Feldpost of 7. Landwehr Division. Another stamp, or Brief-stempel, states "Gerate Kraftwagen-Kolonne Armee-Abtlg. Galde.

Unfortunately, the car cannot be identified as to maker, but the folding rear roof section certainly has to be unusual. The black and white dog belonging to the General staff officer in the rear enjoys the feature. Two Kraftfahrer in caps with goggles and lederrock M1907 tunics are in charge of the vehicle which mounts two Kar 98a's, and a Pionier shovel in side mounts, plus a tri-color fender pennant indicating staff on the front fender.

Five Kraftfahrer in heavy fleece winter coats take a smoke break by the motorpool. The two men on the left wear the issued M1910 visor cap with the larger leather bill; the man in the center wears the standard dienstmütze and ledergamasche gaiters. They are pose in front of a large closed model staff car, with another parked on the right.

A Kraftfahrer in his gray lederrock and hosen, leather jacket and pants and wearing the M1910 drivers visored cap, poses before his huge four-ton NAG truck. Neue Automobil Gesellschaft developed this 60 h.p. general purpose truck from 1909 to 1912. It had Bosch ignition, forced lubrication and a governor to prevent excessive strain on the ample power of the engine. Large numbers of these were built by Daimler, Ehrhardt, and Bussing, as well as NAG, and saw extensive service throughout the war.

A Kraftfahrer on the left is photographed with three staff cars and other military as well as civilian personnel. An NCO wearing an M1915 bluse with collar litzen and an Iron Cross 2nd Class ribbon leans on the fender of a Mercedes staff car with three-pointed stars on each side of the top of the radiator. It is interesting to note that the factories of Mercedes and Benz at the time of World War I were separated by forty miles, Benz and Cie, in Mannheim, Mercedes Daimler-Motoren.Ges in Stuttgart, and they did not merge until 1925. They both built autos and trucks for the German military under their separate names. There were 15 manufacturers who built over 12,000 staff cars for the Imperial Army by 1918.

A Christmas party was in progress when this photograph was taken of a Bavarian unit in rustic quarters. A number of Kraftfahrer appear among this group of men wearing leg-wraps, mountain boots and M1910 tunics with litzen. One driver, standing in the front left, wears a short leather coat with eight bone buttons, while the others are dressed in the M1907 black leather model with silvered buttons.

Twenty-nine Kraftfahrers pose for their unit photograph wearing a variety of uniforms and caps. Most evident are the later war long black leather driving coats with cloth collars and shoulder boards; also seen are M1910 tunics with collar litzen. Headgear consisted of M1912 leather visored caps and M1910 standard issue Dienstmützen and most of those wearing the leather coats also wear driving goggles on their caps. The drivers also wear heavy cleated mountain troop style boots and leg-wraps.

These two Kraftfahrer look quite pleased with themselves posing in a well-maintained Army staff car. They both wear the M1907 lederrock driving coats and M1912 leather driving caps and goggles. The staff car has a forward angle to its windshield, an Imperial Army eagle on the rear door, and a furled staff pennant on the inside of the front fender. Its manufacturer cannot be identified.

Two Kraftfahrers dressed in M1907 lederrock drivers coats are transporting a group of NCOs and men who wear M1910 uniforms and overcoats with litzen on the collars. The truck is a chain-driven NAG (Neue Automobil Gesellschaft) 60 h.p. with solid rubber wheels of a 1909-12 design. A brass horn with a rubber bulb is mounted on the right side by the driver. The reverse is dated 1 February 1916.

This photograph was taken in Lodz, Poland early in December 1915. Two of the Kraftfahrer wear the black M1907 lederrocks and the driver on the left an M1912 leather visor cap. The man behind the wheel wears a heavy fleece driving coat and goggles on his M1910 cap. Two empty rifle racks can be seen just to the rear of the spare tire and before the rear door, plus a pionier shovel can be seen stowed behind the front of the spare. The staff car is thought to be a Stoewer belonging to the Kraftfahrpark of the Gen. Gouv. Warschau. Part of this title appears on the hood and in full on a stamp on the reverse.

Ersatz Pickelhauben M1915

The studio of Jos. Werner in Munich photographed this young Bavarian prior to his departure for the front. His felt ersatz helmet is trimmed in gray metal and bears the Bavarian helmet plate. His uniform consists of an M1910-15 tunic, corduroy trousers, buttoned ledergamasche, or puttees, and M1901 schnürschuh front-laced boots. He is equipped with M1909 patronentaschen ammunition pouches, a M1895 tornister field pack, a Gew 88. and an S71/84 bayonet.

This photo postcard was sent from a training center in Altengrabow on 13 May 1915. The three Prussian infantrymen all wear new M1910 uniforms and the man on the right has been issued a brass-trimmed felt ersatz pickelhaube, the others M1895 leather helmets without field covers. Armed with Gew 98.s and full marching equipment, they were nearing the time for deployment to the front.

Recruit Herzog was photographed in his Prussian brass-trimmed felt ersatz pickelhaube and M1907 overcoat bearing red infantry collar patches and shoulder straps numbered to his regiment, Infantry Regiment Nr. 29. The reverse is dated 30 March 1915 and a Brief Stempel indicates Herzog was part of Rekruten-Depot 2. Ersatz-Batallion Infantry Regiment 29.

Uniforms and Equipment of the Imperial German Army 1900-1918

Five young recruits of the 1st Ersatz Batallion of Infanterie Regiment Nr. 46 and their training NCO were photographed on 22 October 1915 at the depot at Jarotschin. They wear brass-trimmed felt ersatz pickelhauben, M1910 uniforms and are armed with Gew 98.s.

A close look at the older age of these men indicates their status as members of the Baden 1st Landsturm Infanterie Batallion, Freiburg, 8th Landwehr Division. They have been recalled for service and all but one wear brass-trimmed felt ersatz pickelhauben with the Baden frontplate; the man on the far right wears an M1895 leather helmet also trimmed in brass. A feldwebel in a M1915 bluse holding a sword is in the center of the photograph, as well as the cook in his white apron. The rest of the troops wear M1910 uniforms and are armed with Gew 88.s and S71 bayonets.

137

Uniforms and Equipment of the Imperial German Army 1900-1918

This Prussian infantryman has been issued a variation of the ersatz felt pickelhaube with brass trim, but also with an extra gray leather trim piece around the edge of the helmet. He is photographed in his M1910 uniform, M1909 patronentaschen, M1895 tornister pack and a Gew 71/84. rifle.

Another variation is pictured of the felt ersatz pickelhaube which in this case had no edge trim applied to this brass-trimmed specimen. Our infantryman is otherwise equipped with the standard M1910 uniform, field equipment and a Gew 98. with an ersatz bayonet.

"A faithful watch at Christmas in the Argonne 1915" is the title of this photograph. Two fur-clad and bearded sentries of the 34th Infantrie Division holding Gew 98.s are on alert duty. The man on the left wears an uncovered brass-trimmed felt ersatz pickelhaube which seems strange when in a forward position; his companion wears his helmet covered. The reverse is postmarked 21 December 1915.

This photograph is in memory of the swearing in of these six young recruits into the 2nd Ersatz Batallion of Infanterie Regiment Nr. 166 on 1 June 1915. All are issued brass-trimmed felt ersatz pickelhauben with brass trim on the front visors, and M1910 tunics with corduroy trousers. Only two of the tunics bear shoulder straps which are both marked with chainstitched "166".

A serious young Baden infantryman in a studio photograph with a tennis court backdrop. His brass-trimmed ersatz felt pickelhaube bears the Baden griffin frontplate and looks brand new, as does his M1910 uniform.

A Prussian infantryman poses in an urban setting wearing an ersatz felt pickelhaube with brass trim and a Prussian eagle frontplate. He wears an M1910 uniform and is armed with a Gew 88. with an S71 bayonet.

Recent recruits of Landwehr Infanterie Regiment Nr. 83 are pictured with their two NCOs in M1910 uniforms while they wear the training M1895 uniforms. The two fully equipped men standing on the extreme left and right wear stamped tin ersatz gray helmets which appear to have brass fittings, and are armed with Gew 88. rifles with S71 bayonets. Also seen in the photograph are musicians with bugles, and a drummer with drum and drum hanger on his belt.

An interesting photograph of five newly-trained infantrymen from Landwehr Infantry Regiment Nr. 72 with the traditional sprigs of flowers ready to depart for the front. They are all equipped with felt brass-trimmed ersatz pickelhauben, fresh M1910 uniforms, full marching gear, and are armed with Gew 88.s with ersatz bayonets. Their training NCOs stand in the rear center, one wearing a Litewka-style tunic and a marksman's lanyard, and the other an M1895 uniform with NCO collar discs. The real mystery about this photo is the ownership of the pair of M1893 schnürschuh side-laced boots by the door on the right.

A Bavarian Landsturm infantryman was photographed wearing an ersatz felt pickelhaube with a brass Bavarian frontplate and an M1910/15 uniform. His uniform bears shoulder straps of webbing material and the brass number 9 on his collar. He is equipped with M1909 patronentaschen ammunition boxes, a breadbag over his shoulder and a Gew 88. with a S71/04 bayonet. A letter on the reverse is dated 8 May 1915.

Dresden was the location of the Knees Studio where this soldier from Prussian Infanterie Regiment Nr. 3 posed for his portrait. He wears a brass-trimmed ersatz felt pickelhaube, with a gray leather edge binding not commonly seen. In this clear photograph we can see his M1907 overcoat with red collar patches and the shoulder straps bearing the chainstitched number "3", as well as his schnürschuh M1893 side-laced shoes.

In this photograph four variations of the ersatz pickelhaube can be seen. They are the gray felt version with no edge trim, the gray felt version with brass visor trim, the black pressed metal version with brass visor trim and the black pressed metal version with no trim. All men are dressed in the same M1910 uniforms, but are armed with a variety of Gew 71/84. and Gew 98. rifles.

Members of the 1st Ersatz Batallion of Saxon Infantry Regiment Nr. 139 are photographed in 1915 by the Böttger Studio near their Kasern in Döbeln. Four ersatz felt pickelhauben with Saxon frontplates and brass trim are clearly visible being worn by musketiers armed with Gew 98.s.

This Prussian infantryman and his wife were photographed in February 1915 and a notation on the reverse states he was killed in action on 15 July 1915. At the time of the photograph, he was wearing a Prussian ersatz felt brass-trimmed pickelhaube, a fresh M1910 uniform and M1893 side-laced shoes.

Training has been completed by this young Bavarian infantryman, and wearing the symbolic flowers, he is about to depart to join his regiment. He wears a felt ersatz helmet with a Bavarian frontplate and visor trim in brass, an M1910/15 uniform and light brown field equipment. It is interesting to see the color contrast between the gray of his tunic and that of his trousers. The reverse is postmarked Regensburg, 10 March 1915.

Another variation of the ersatz pickelhaube is seen in this photograph of a Prussian infantryman in training. This helmet variation is of pressed lightweight metal with gray painted metal fittings rather than brass. Our subject is dressed in an M1895 tunic used for training and an elderly Gew 71/84. was his weapon.

BELOW: The training center at Juterbog was the location of Ernst Löhn, the photographer who took this photograph of a reserve unit and their training NCOs. They wear a variety of ersatz pickelhauben, felt with brass-trim, with and without visor trim, and pressed light metal with gray metal fittings, with and without visor trim. The Feldwebel stripes on the arm of the man in the center can be seen, as well as the extra tressing on the collars and cuffs of the 1st Sergeant to his right.

Uniforms and Equipment of the Imperial German Army 1900-1918

Cavalry - Dragoons

A trooper of Prussian Dragoon Regiment Nr. 26, with a large symbolic bouquet, leaves for the front. He is dressed in an M1910 uniform, M1895 pickelhaube with a field cover and brass-scaled chinstrap and tall cavalry boots. He is armed with a Kar 98a slung on his back and an M1889 cavalry sword. All appropriate cavalry equipment of M1895-1911 pattern is in view, including the lance bucket on his stirrup. He carries his sword in the position often reserved for the carbine in its leather scabbard. The reverse of the photo postcard is dated Saarburg 7 February 1915.

Five troopers from Württemberg Reserve Dragoon Regiment Nr. 5 pose in their covered square-visored Dragoon helmets with field covers, M1910 tunics and cavalry riding breeches with leather reinforced inner legs. They were issued M1911 patronentaschen cavalry-style ammunition pouches supported by leather Y-straps, tall cavalry boots and Kar 98a carbines.

Dragoons from Württemberg Dragoon Regiment Nr. 25 Köningin Olga form a firing line with their Kar 98a's at the ready. They are dressed in M1910 uniforms with collar and cuff litzen and cyphered shoulder straps of the regiment and covered Dragoon-style pickelhauben. The bayonets mounted on the Kar 98a's were altered S71/84s which were designed to fit this rifle.

Five troopers from the Baden Leib-Dragoon Regiment Nr. 20 pose for a group portrait by Jakob Kofman of Karlsruhe which was the garrison city of the 20th. They wear M1910 tunics with the red crown cypher of the regiment on their shoulder straps, tall cavalry boots, open buckle cavalry belts, dark, leather reinforced riding breeches and gray mützen with red bands.

A group photograph of the 2nd Landsturm Eskadron of Dragoon Regiment Köningin Olga (1. Württemberg) Nr. 25 with a quantity of detail worth study. The date of the picture is October 1914, taken by K. Hils Studio in Ludwigsburg, the regiment's garrison city. They are dressed in M1895 light blue, trimmed in white, tunics with litzen on the collars, Württemberg Dragoon-style pickelhauben with reserve crosses on the helmet plates, some with white dress belts, some in brown leather, some in riding breeches and tall boots, some in cotton drill stable uniforms, and those without helmets wear blue and white mützen with the Württemberg lower cockade. Weapons consist of a Kar 88. carbine and M1889 cavalry sabers. Two trumpeters stand in the rear row center.

ABOVE: A guard mount of six troopers and an NCO of the 2. Badisches-Dragoner-Regiment Nr. 21 pose at the present arms position. They all wear the M1895 light blue with red trim uniforms, square-cut visor Dragoon pickelhauben with the Baden griffin frontplate, white dress belts and cartouche box straps, riding breeches and tall cavalry boots. The troopers are armed with both Kar 98a rifles and M1889 cavalry sabers; the NCO carries the sword only. The reverse bears a postmark of Bruchsal the home of 1., 2., 3., and 5. Eskadron of the 21st and dated 21 November 1909.

An NCO from one of the Garde Dragoon regiments poses wearing his M1910 tunic and field service cap, brown cavalry field belt and the ribbon of the Iron Cross 1st Class.

A trooper from Dragoon Regiment Köningin Olga (1. Württemberg) Nr. 25 stands for his formal portrait at a Ludwigsburg studio. He is dressed in his walking-out uniform, M1895 tunic, black straight leg trousers, black dress belt, blue and white visor cap, white gloves and an M1889 cavalry saber with the Württemberg coat of arms worked into the hilt.

Dragooner Herrmann, 5. Eskadron, 3. Schlesisches Dragoon-Regiment Nr. 15, 7. Kav. Division is photographed in his M1910 tunic, riding breeches, tall cavalry boots, brown cavalry service belt and a riding crop for effect. The reverse is dated 6 October 1915 and Feldpost stamped K.B. 1. Landwehr-Division.

Cavalry - Bavarian Chavaulegers

A 1918 photograph of a Bavarian NCO Chavauleger (Light Horse) who served with the 8. Chavaulegers Regiment. He poses in an M1910/15 Chavauleger tunic with white piping and a red numeral "8" on the shoulder straps. As can be seen, these Bavarian tunics were piped only on one side of the double row of buttons found on the chest, while Ulans from the other states and Prussia had piping on both sides of the chest. Riding breeches with ledergamasche leggings and laced boots and a white-piped visor cap complete his uniform. He is wearing the ribbons for two Bavarian awards and the Iron Cross 2nd Class.

A post-1914 photograph of Bavarian Chavauleger recruit trainees wearing the M1895 dark green and red training uniforms. They wear M1909 patronentasche ammunition pouches supported by cavalry-style leather "Y" straps, cavalry open buckle belts, mounted troops boots and entrenching tools are worn by some on the right. Close inspection shows piping only on the buttoning edge of their tunics.

A particularly interesting photograph of dismounted Bavarian Chavaulegers in varying equipment. A field-covered pickelhaube and a gas mask container are worn by the trooper on the far right; M1916 Stahlhelm are worn by the trooper on the far left and one standing near the center. All pertinent cavalry equipment can be seen, lances, Kar 98a's in leather scabbards, saddles and saddle bags, and bridles are visible.

A Bavarian Chavauleger sergeant poses for his formal portrait wearing an M1910 ulanka with the single piped front, service cavalry belt with a holstered pistol under his right arm, leather reinforced riding breeches, leg-wraps and schnürschuh front-laced boots with spurs. On the table rests his dienstmütze visor cap with piping to his regiment.

Bavarians all: an infantryman wearing an M1910/15 tunic and corduroy trousers, a woman who appears to be dressed as a tram, or bus conductor, and a Chavauleger in his M1910 tunic, leather reinforced riding breeches and cavalry boots with spurs.

Uniforms and Equipment of the Imperial German Army 1900-1918

Proud Bavarian Chavauleger NCO Jacob Wittmann sits astride his charger on 29 March 1917. He carries a riding crop and wears an M1910/15 tunic in this field photograph.

Christmas found these six Bavarian Chavaulegers NCOs in a rather pensive mood. They all have been decorated with Bavarian awards and some with the Iron Cross 2nd Class. Their tunics are of the M1910/15 pattern and they wear a variety of cavalry boots and ledergamasche with their riding breeches. One man wears what appears to be an undress stable jacket.

Rauchmillers Studio in Sünzburg on the Danube took this photograph of three Bavarians in 1916. The man on the right is a Chavauleger wearing an M1910 tunic, cavalry belt, boots and a mütze cap with a large Bavarian State cocarde.

An infantryman from Bavarian Infantry Regiment Nr. 2 and a Chavauleger from Bavarian Chavaulegers Regiment Nr. 6 are photographed in Posen on 15 June 1916. The 6. Chavaulegers-Regiment Prinz Ubrecht V. Preussen wore light red piping on the tunic and on the band of the mütze. Our subject wears the M1910 tunic, riding breeches and cavalry belt and boots.

A mounted Bavarian Chavauleger NCO without field equipment poses for a sunny day portrait. He wears his regimentally-piped visor cap and his M1910 tunic, ribbon bar, cavalry belt and holstered pistol.

Two Bavarian troopers of 3. Chavaulegers-Regiment Herzog Karl Theodor take a break in the field for this picture. The man on the left wears the ribbon of the Bavarian Military Service Cross on his M1910 tunic which is piped in light red and the other wears a black mourning band with an Iron Cross for a family member killed in action.

Cavalry - Jäger zu Pferde

A fine studio portrait of a Jäger zu Pferde (literally hunter on horseback) wearing the distinctive green gray colored M1910/15 tunic, riding breeches, cavalry boots, cavalry service belt and mütze with a green band. The sword he is holding appears to be a mounted artillery type, but the position of his hands makes it difficult to determine positively.

Uniforms and Equipment of the Imperial German Army 1900-1918

An unusual combination of Jäger zu Pferde and Kraftfahrer troops posing by a damaged bunker complex near the front lines. The Jäger zu Pferde troopers wear M1910 Waffenrocks; the one on the left carries a fencing proficiency chevron on the sleeve, tall cavalry boots and spurs. The Kraftfahrer drivers wear the M1907 black leather uniforms; the one on the right has a leather visor cap and a bayonet.

A Jäger zu Pferde, 2nd from left, a Dragoon next to him and two flanking Landesgendarmerie all wearing the gorget badge of authority as Feldgendarmerie, or field police, pose in a rural setting. All wear mounted-style boots, holstered pistols and the Jäger zu Pferde carries a sword. The reverse has a long message and the date 12 September 1916.

Cavalry - Ulans

An Ulan lancer from Ulan Regiment Graf Dohna (Ostpreuss) Nr. 8 in a studio posed late in the war. His M1910 ulanka tunic bears pear-shaped shoulder straps with a red chainstitched "8" and is piped in blue, as was the rest of the tunic. His tschapska helmet is of gray felt and with brass fittings. He was equipped with cavalry breeches with reinforced thighs, tall cavalry boots, and infantry model belt and an S14 bayonet, but no sword. Ulans late in the war were converted to foot assault troops which may explain the belt and bayonet.

Lt. Matthias von Borke of 2. Pomm. Ulanen-Regiment Nr. 9 is photographed with his faithful mount. His visor cap and ulanka are piped in white and are both M1910. The reverse bears the date 8 May 1916.

Uniforms and Equipment of the Imperial German Army 1900-1918

A sentimental commercial postcard depicts a Garde Ulan and his loved one. Ulanen-Treue, (Ulan fidelity) is the message at the top of the photograph and this card was sent by Ulan Heize, III Garde Ulan Regiment, Potsdam to his lady friend on 30 October 1916.

Gen. Feldmarschall Graf von Haeseler was the oldest serving general in the German Army during the 1914-18 War. He was the Chef of Ulanen-Regiment Graf Haesler (2. Brandenburgisches) - Nr. 11 and is shown wearing the Ulan uniform in this commercial postcard by Gustav Liersch of Berlin. The reverse shows it was sent from Stuttgart to Newark, New Jersey during the earlier part of the War.

Two brothers-in-arms meet to be photographed in Flanders 15 July 1918. The man on the right is an Ulan from 2. Hannov. Ulan Regiment Nr. 14 who is pictured in his M1910 ulanka piped in red, visor cap, corduroy riding breeches and tall cavalry boots with spurs. His companion is in a M1915 Feldbluse, mütze, leg-wraps and schnürschuh M1901 front-laced shoes.

A Württemberg Ulan from the 10th or 19th Ulan Regiment had his portrait taken by the Grosskopf Studio in Aalen. His M1910 ulanka and mütze are trimmed in red, his riding breeches are of heavy twill and he wears woolen leg-wraps, dress shoes and spurs.

An early war photograph of five Ulanen from the Thüringisches Ulanen-Regiment Nr. 6 from Hanau taken 21 December 1914. They are all dressed in M1910 red-piped ulankas with pear-shaped cyphered shoulder straps, leather reinforced riding breeches, tall boots, cavalry field belts, cavalry-style patronentaschen cartridge boxes and tschapskas with no field covers which was unusual. Weapons were Kar 88. carbines and M1889 cavalry sabers.

A mounted and fully-equipped Ulan, Hugo Listz, of the Kgl. Sächs. 2. Ulanen-Regiment Nr. 18 was photographed in Halloville on 23 April 1916. This exceptionally clear picture shows in detail the cavalry tack and method of carrying the saddle bags, overcoat blanket, lance and Kar 98a. Listz wears a Saxon-style ulanka with square-cut shoulder straps, rather than pear-shaped, piped in red as is the ulanka, a field-covered tschapska M1895 with a brass-scaled chinstrap, Kavallerie-Reithosen riding breeches and tall boots. His lance is of steel and the four buttons near the tip are for attaching Lanzenflagges, or pennants.

Dressed for parade, these two 3rd Garde Ulanen Regiment troopers posed for Berlin photographer Schubert in September of 1908. They wear blue M1895 ulankas trimmed in yellow, cap lines with decorative flounder ends, silver-trimmed tschapskas and epaulets. Weapons consisted of Kar 98a's in leather scabbards, M1889 cavalry sabers, and metal lances with pennants.

A mounted parade of 2. Garde-Ulanen Regiment from Berlin pass before steel-helmeted troops on 27 January 1918. They wear covered tschapskas, M1907 cavalry overcoats and carry lances with black and white pennants. The exact location of the review cannot be determined.

An Ulan from Ulanen-Rgt. König Wilhelm I (2. Württem.) Nr. 20 strikes a heroic pose for the photographer. His M1910/15 ulanka is piped in yellow as are his shoulder straps which bear the crown over "W" cypher of the regiment in red. His tschapska is covered, but the red and black feldabzeichen of Württemberg can be seen on the edge of the mortar board top of his helmet. Cavalry-style support straps hold the M1909 patronentaschen pouches in position and his armament consists of a Kar 98a and an M1889 cavalry saber with the Württemberg arms worked into the hilt.

Unfortunately, the exact regiment of this Prussian Ulan trooper cannot be determined from this photograph. He is beautifully mounted on a dapple gray horse wearing a covered tschapska with a Prussian abzeichen, a M1910 ulanka and interestingly, an infantry-style belt and buckle supporting his M1889 cavalry saber.

Three Ulanen and their mounts from König Sachs. 3. Ulanen-Regiment Nr. 21 (Kaiser Wilhelm II König v. Preussen) pose in the field for photographer Otto Dubielzig from Munster, home of the XIII cavalry division. They are wearing the M1910 ulanka with yellow piping, square cut shoulder straps also piped in yellow with red crown over "W" cyphers, covered M1895 tschapskas with exposed Prussian abzeichen and cavalry-style patronentaschen and supporting straps.

A winter scene of four Ulanen and their mounts on patrol. Their cavalry-style mantel overcoats bear Garde litzen and numbered shoulder straps which make a strange combination as the first numeral is 2. The 21st Ulanen Regiment wore litzen, but with cyphered straps that were not numbered. The trooper on foot is armed with a Kar 88. carbine slung over his shoulder.

Uniforms and Equipment of the Imperial German Army 1900-1918

Two of these Ulan NCOs, 2nd and 3rd from the left, wear newly presented Iron Crosses 2nd Class suspended from their issue ribbons. The card was produced in France and the reverse bears a handwritten date of October 1914. They all wear M1910 ulanka tunics and covered M1895 tschapskas with chinstraps in the lowered position. The specific regiment is unknown.

A mounted patrol of Ulanen are photographed with lances flying the black and white enlisted pennants and the NCO pennants which carry the Imperial eagle. They are dressed in M1910 tunics and felt brass-trimmed ersatz tschapskas with brass-scaled chinstraps and Prussian abzeichen. The photograph was taken by E. Löhn, with studios in Berlin and Juterbog, and the reverse shows a Juterbog postmark.

An Ulan and friend are photographed in France standing by an ornately decorated building, the effigy of a lion behind them. The Ulan is wearing his M1910 ulanka with what appears to be yellow piping and plain yellow-piped pear-shaped shoulder boards which would indicate 3. Garde-Ulanen Regiment, but there is no Garde collar litzen and a brass line eagle is on his felt ersatz tschapska. Further from the norm are his leg-wraps and laced and polished shoes. His sword is of the M1889 cavalry pattern and his NCO friend carries an S71/84 bayonet and wears mounted troop boots with his M1910 tunic.

A 2. Garde Ulanen-Regiment NCO was photographed in Ghent, Belgium sometime during the summer of 1915. His wears the walking-out uniform of an M1910 red-piped ulanka with Garde litzen on the collar and cuffs, straight leg trousers and M1893 side-laced schnürschuh, or shoes. His sword is patterned after the French "Chasseur" saber and was carried by Ulans before being replaced by the M1889 pattern.

Ulans and other German forces escorting captured French infantry to captivity through the streets of Lille early July 1915. The two Ulanen in the foreground carry their lances with the pennants furled and Kar 98a's slung over their shoulders. The unit is Prussian, but the regiment cannot be determined. A letter on the reverse is dated 4 July 1915.

A company of Ulanen being led by their NCOs ride through the village of Nauheim. They are dressed in cavalry-style mantels, or overcoats, and mützen, rather than helmets and are carrying full equipment on their horses, including lances with furled pennants.

Uniforms and Equipment of the Imperial German Army 1900-1918

This photograph should have been used for a recruiting poster for the Ulanen Regiments. The clear focused detail of all the equipment and uniform of this NCO is quite remarkable. The dapple gray horse with his cropped mane appears to be carefully groomed and cared for. Our man wears his M1910 ulanka, dark riding breeches, tall cavalry boots and spurs, and covered M1895 tschapska with a Prussian abzeichen. His equipment consists of cavalry straps supporting his ammunition pouches, open buckled cavalry field belt, M1889 saber, Kar 98a, M1890 stahlrohrlanze with furled pennant, saddle bags and large mess tin in its leather case.

On the 25th of January 1918 this trooper from Ulan-Regiment König Karl (1. Württemb.) Nr. 19 was serving as a bicycle messenger. He wears an M1910 ulanka with collar litzen and cyphered pear-shaped shoulder straps, mounted breeches, cavalry boots and a message pouch suspended from his service cavalry belt. Quite a change from the preceding photograph.

By mid-1917 the roles of cavalry had changed as can be seen in this picture of a group of Ulanen from the 6th or 19th Ulans wearing steel M1916 helmets, carrying gas masks and with their feet on the ground, not in stirrups. The Briefstempel on the reverse indicates 2. Inf. Pl. Ko. Landwehr Infantry Regiment Nr. 120 and the date of 23 August 1917.

An Ulan officer on staff greets a party of visiting dignitaries, including a general, by a headquarters building. Behind him is a Saxon officer saluting and a guard mount of infantry wearing M1910 uniforms armed with Gew 88. rifles with S72 bayonets. Note the double-wide red stripes on the general's breeches.

A gala Ulan wedding party poses in the Kaserne courtyard in Saarburg. The groom, wearing full dress including the colored plastron, or bib, on the front of the ulanka, is in the center without a helmet and wears a white dress belt across his chest supporting a decorative cartouche box, three fencing proficiency stripes on his arm and the flounders from his cap lines on his left chest. Ulan regular and field grade officers, a Dragoon officer, an Infantry officer and many ranking Ulan NCOs make up the military part of the wedding party, while numerous gentlemen in top-hats and morning coats, with their ladies, make up the civilian portion. Unfortunately, the regiment cannot be identified, but the occasion was one of importance judging from the attendees.

A combination of uniforms can be seen in this posed photograph of four service men. Front row left is an Ulan of the 11th or 15th Regiment, who wore yellow facings wearing his M1895 blue ulanka, visor cap, straight leg trousers which were strapped under his dress boots which carried spurs. He holds a fine example of a M1889 cavalry saber. Seated on his right is a Feld-Artillerie Kanonier wearing his M1895 dress blue, trimmed with black, uniform. He is equipped with a mounted troops belt and a mounted artillery sword. Standing left, an infantryman wearing a M1910/15 feldgrau tunic and next to him another infantryman of Hannoverian Infantry Regiment Nr. 164 in his M1895 blue uniform.

Another mixed group posed in 1914 in the studio of J. Lemaire of Namur, Belgium. On the right is an NCO of Württemberg Ulan Regiment Nr. 19 wearing the collar and cuff litzen of that regiment and holding a M1889 cavalry saber. Next to him is seated an NCO of Württemberg Grenadier Regiment Nr. 123 wearing his M1910 uniform with the cyphered shoulder straps of his regiment. The other two men are Kanonier from Württemberg Reserve Fuss Artillerie Regiment Nr. 13 as indicated by the metal numerals "13" on their shoulder straps.

ABOVE: Herr Voss from Dörnitz traveled to the Kaserne in Altin-Grabow, home of IV Armee Korps, in 1906 to photograph this mixed group of military types. Standing left we see an Ulan in full dress, standing right a Jäger zu Pferde in a mütze, dress tunic, work trousers and high cavalry boots. Two other Ulans are seated in ulankas, plus one additional Jäger zu Pferde, a civilian and three members of Infantry Regiment Nr. 5.

An from Württemberg Ulan Regiment Nr. 19 wearing his M1910 uniform with collar and cuff litzen, cavalry field belt and mütze poses with a powerfully built Württemberg infantryman clad in a M1910/15 uniform. The date and place are unknown.

Cavalry - Kürassiere

A Kürassier from Leib-Kürassier-Regiment Grosser Kurfürst Nr. 1. in full dress is photographed by the W. Probst Studio of Breslau, the garrison town of the regiment. His tunic is dark blue with black collar and cuffs piped in white. The polished Kürassier helm bears an eagle helmet plate with a banner stating "Pro Glorie Et Patria", the eagle being in a different attitude of flight from a line eagle making the plate unique to this regiment. The ringkragen, or gorget, worn by this trooper is the mannschaft, or enlisted man's, style which lacks the enameling in the center found on examples of the NCO and officer's types. The three regiments authorized to wear gorgets were the Garde du Corps, Kürassier-Regiment Nr. 1, and Kürassier Regiment Nr. 2. and each had a pattern of its own. Our man shows a white cartouche box cross strap and white dress sword belt for the mannschafts-pollasch heavy saber which he holds before him. White breeches and tall polished cavalry boots and spurs complete his outfit. The two young women are not identified, but certainly are smartly turned out for this 25 October 1914 occasion.

A sharp contrast from the preceding photograph is seen in this view of a Kürassier from Kürassier-Regiment Nr. 5. taken 2 October 1916. The M1910 Waffenrock with Kürassier borte, or tape, on the collar and cuffs is worn with a visor cap both which carry piping and trim in the rose red color of the Regiment. Also seen are cavalry breeches and the tall Kürassier-style boots and spurs. A brown cavalry field belt supports an S71/84 bayonet issued to cavalry for the Kar 98a. The Brief-stempel postmark on the reverse states Mobile Landwehr-Eskadron XX AK (20th Armee Korps).

Uniforms and Equipment of the Imperial German Army 1900-1918

These four Kürassiere were photographed in Brussels on 30 October 1915 in full parade dress. Pre-war brass-trimmed Kürassier helmets, white koller tunics and breeches, white dress sword and cartouche belts, high-fronted cavalry boots and Kürassier swords were the uniform of the day. As can be seen by the schwalbennester decorations on their shoulders, they are all trumpeter musicians.

Nine troopers of Kürassier-Regiment Königin (Pommersches) Nr. 2 in parade Kollers, Ringkagen M1895 gorgets, brass-trimmed Kürassier helmets, high boots and lances were in attendance at a special occasion in Cöslin. The nature of the occasion is unknown, but the attendees are an interesting mixture of a police official on the far left, civilians, men, women and children and what appears to be an elderly bearded officer in uniform.

177

This young Kürassier was photographed 8 April 1916 while attached to the 9th Company, Reserve Infantry Regiment Nr. 71 of the 22nd Reserve Division. He is wearing a M1910/15 Waffenrock with Kürassier borte, or decorative tape, on the collar and sewn-in shoulder straps. An open buckle cavalry belt supports an S98/05 bayonet on his hip and reinforced riding breeches complete his uniform. At the time this photo was taken he was in all probability serving as dismounted cavalry. Note his pocket watch worn in a special strap on his wrist.

A heavy cavalry trooper from the Bavarian Schwere Reiter Regiment is photographed wearing the Bavarian M1910/15 tunic, riding breeches, cavalry boots and spurs, and a field-covered pickelhaube as worn by the two Schwere Reiter Regiments. Suspended from his cavalry field belt is a Bavarian heavy cavalry saber. A notation on the reverse indicates the subject was Seyfried Adolf who died 8 June 1949.

Uniforms and Equipment of the Imperial German Army 1900-1918

A trooper from the Saxon Karabinier Regiment (2. Schweres Regt.) is photographed in his dress blue, with black collar and cuffs Waffenrock. He also wears a white-topped visor cap with a gray wartime visor, feldgrau straight leg trousers, white dress belt, gray gloves and an M89 cavalry sword with a folding hilt.

A Kürassier reserve officer was photographed wearing the dress Kürassier helmet with a reserve cross on the frontplate, cavalry officers mantel with the ribbon of the Iron Cross 2nd Class through the second buttonhole, dress cavalry boots and spurs, and is armed with the Kürassier officers pallasch. The photograph is dated Brussels 1917.

BELOW: A troop of Kürassier Regiment Nr. 7 pose for Halberstadt photographer Otto Harder in March of 1912. The service uniform of the 7th was blue with yellow trim and the parade uniform was white with yellow trim. In this photograph we see both uniforms, plus two mounted troopers in parade dress with the Kürass, or upper body armor, and lances. The early film plays a trick on the eye by making yellow appear to be a dark color, as seen in this photograph.

Cavalry - Husaren

An NCO of an unidentified Prussian Husar regiment was preparing to board a railcar in this 1915 dated photograph. He wears a pre-war Pelzmütze with a brass-scaled chinstrap, black and white feldabzeichen and gray field cover, an M1910 attila with corded frogging and trim with an NCO collar disc. Reinforced riding breeches and tall cavalry boots with metal toe protectors round out his uniform. Equipment consisted of M1911 cavalry patronentaschen, M1911 leather supporting "Y" straps, cavalry field belt and a Kar 98a. A fine study of a wartime Husar.

Another view of the same man holding his M1889 cavalry sword and clearly displaying the striped one-year volunteer shoulder straps.

A one-year volunteer from Husaren-Regiment v. Zieten (Brandenburgisches) Nr. 3 poses for a carte-de-visite wearing a red attila with white trim, Lange Hosen für Husaren, tight fitting trousers and Husar boots with silver trim. His mütze of cavalry-style is red with a blue band and white trim. The carte-de-visite was taken by the Steinberger and Bauer studio in Frankfurt.

General von Kavaliere Adolf Wilhelm Victor, Prinz zu Schaumburg-Lippe in the uniform of the Husaren-Regiment König Wilhelm I (1. Rheinisches) Nr. 7. The attila of the 7th was Russian blue with gold frogging and lace. His Pelzmütze is of opossum fur with a red Kolpack, or bag, and the unique badge of the 7th, a crown over the cypher of Wilhelm I. The sword he holds is Kavallerie-Offiziersäbel M1892.

An informal inspection is being conducted of the troops of Husaren-Regiment Nr. 7 on 9 August 1914. A mixture of dress and fatigue uniforms is worn; litewkas, stable jackets, attila's, visor caps, Pelzmützen with the regimental cypher and the distinctive Husar boots are all in evidence. The NCO in the cotton drill trousers holds an M1889 cavalry sword while the first sergeant in the background makes notes in his order book. The attila worn by the 7th was medium blue in color with yellow cording and the bag on the Pelzmütze was red.

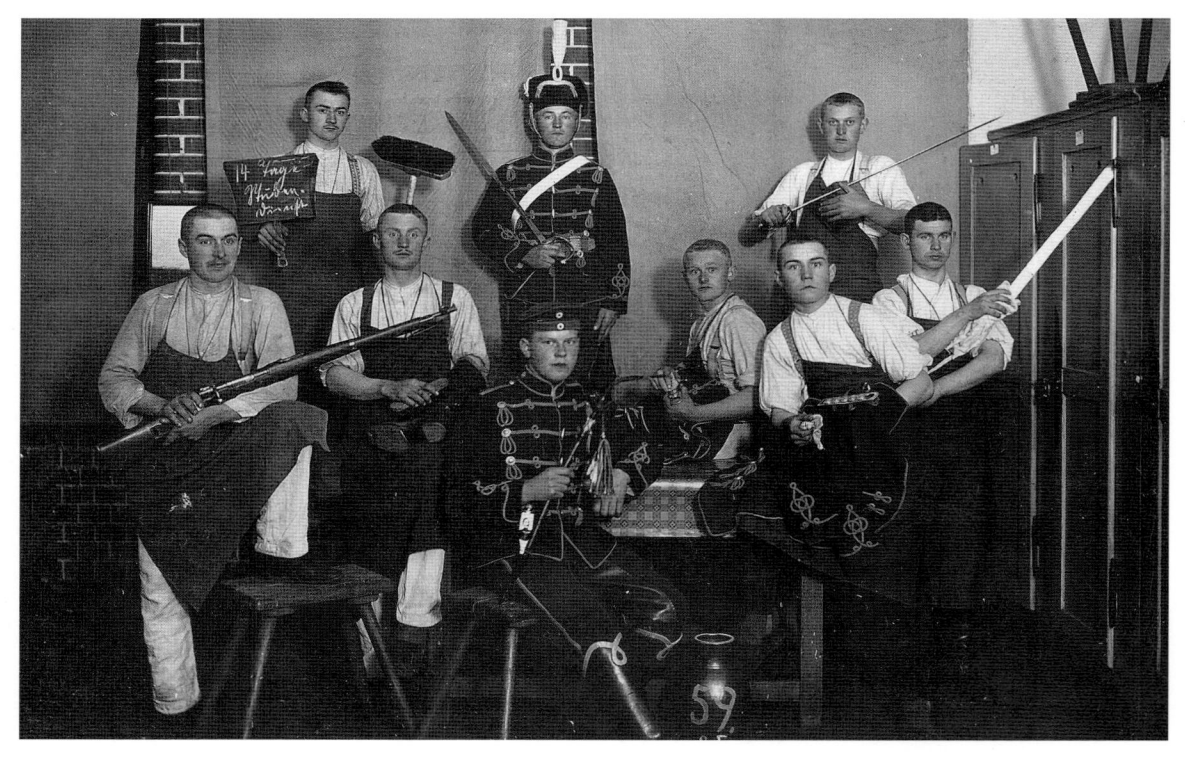

A wonderful occupational photo of nine members of the Magdeburgisches Husaren-Regiment Nr. 10 in their barracks room at Stendal, the regiment's garrison town. The duties being performed from left to right are cleaning the Kar 98a, sweeping the area with dustpan and broom, boot polishing, standing parade guard, sitting, relaxing and smoking a patriotic decorated pipe, polishing buttons with the device used to protect the attila from polish stains, cleaning the M1889 sword and finally, whitening the dress belting. The attila's of the 10th Husars were dark green with gold cording trim and the Pelzmützen were black sealskin with pompadour red bags. The reverse bears the date 8 December 1913.

Uniforms and Equipment of the Imperial German Army 1900-1918

A studio-posed photograph of a Husar from the Husaren-Regiment Graf Goetzen Nr. 6 in full field equipment. He wears the feldgrau M1910 attila, a Pelzmütze with field cover, cavalry "Y" support straps, M1911 cavalry patronentaschen ammunition pouches, Husar-style boots with spurs, and a Kar 98a carbine. The reverse bears a Feldpost stamp "3 Kavallerie Division 6.H".

A Husar Feldwebel poses for his photograph in front of a hewn log house on the Eastern front in 1915. He is dressed in an M1910/15 attila with plain cuffs, an M1910 field service cap, reinforced cavalry breeches, cavalry boots and spurs. He had been awarded the Iron Cross 2nd Class as seen by the ribbon in his second buttonhole.

185

Uniforms and Equipment of the Imperial German Army 1900-1918

A Landsturm Husar from the 6. Landsturm Cavalry Division at Ottenstein is photographed in August of 1915, mounted and ready for action. His Pelzmütze carries a field cover and the later period leather, rather than scaled brass, chinstrap and the Prussian feldabzeichen. He wears an M1910 attila in combination with the earlier dark M1895 Husar breeches, undecorated Husar boots, M1911 cavalry patronentaschen ammo boxes and M1911 leather supporting straps. His armament consists of an M1890 lance with a black and white enlisted pennant, an M1889 cavalry sword and a Kar 88. carbine. The socket for the lance butt is by his left stirrup.

Another interior view of the Magdeburgisches Husaren-Regiment Nr. 10 at their Kasern in Stendal. The date of the photograph is 27 February 1912 and shows troopers in their dark green, gold-trimmed attilas, stable dress, litewkas, aprons, and dark vests. Headgear ranges from M1895 Pelzmützen with bags in what was called "pompadour" red to mützen of two styles, one of the standard style and one in the cavalry-style of a wider top and extended by a stiffener. A trooper on chimney sweep duty is on the left, while others polish boots and swords, stand ready for guard duty, hold food dishes and just relax. The M1889 cavalry swords and the Pelzmütze in the center are a nice touch.

An unfortunately faded rare photograph of a trooper from Braunschweigisches Husaren-Regiment Nr. 17. His Pelzmütze is made of bearskin, while those of all other Husar regiments were made of sealskin. The mützenbeutel, or cap bag, was of red material and the skull and crossbones frontplate was unique to the 17th. In the Napoleonic Wars the Brunswick troops fought with the British, and the 17th Duke of Cambridge's Own Lancers used the identical insignia. He wears the M1910 gray attila, brown cavalry field belt, Husar breeches, with leg-wraps and front-laced low quarter boots M1901. The reverse is dated 15 April 1916 and carries the Feldpost stamp of the 19. Inf. Div.

Two Husaren from the reserves of 2. Rheinisches Husaren-Regiment Nr. 9 pose for this informal photograph on 20 May 1916. They are both wearing mütze caps, M1910/15 attilas, mounted breeches, and one man favors legwraps and M1901 front-laced boots and the other tall cavalry boots, but not of the Husar type. The reverse bears two stamps, one for the 9. Res. Hus. Rgt. and the other for the 30. Reserve Div.

A photograph taken in the field of a Husar NCO from an unidentified regiment. He poses in an M1910 attila, M1910 visor field cap, Husar breeches, leg-wraps and cleated mountain boots. The cane, the Fernglas 08 binoculars, and a P. 08 Luger on his hip give him the look of a serving front-line soldier.

A dapper Prussian Feldwebel Husar poses wearing an M1910 attila with NCO collar discs, plus NCO tressing on the collar and cuffs, early-style Husar breeches with white stripes on the legs and high cavalry-style boots and spurs.

Husar Hugo Krekel on the right and three friends enjoy a smoke while posing for their photograph at a studio somewhere in France. They are all wearing mützen, M1910 attilas, Husar breeches and Husar decorated boots. The trooper on the left has been awarded a fencing proficiency chevron which he wears on his right sleeve. Note how short-waisted the attila actually was.

A worn and scratched but worthy photograph of a Husar NCO from 2. Husaren-Regiment Nr. 19 Kronprinz Wilhelm des Deutschen Reiches und von Preussen taken 23 April 1915. He had recently been awarded the Iron Cross 2nd Class which he wears in the button hole of an M1910 attila with NCO collar discs and tressing. He is armed with an M1890/93 lance without a pennant and an M1889 cavalry sword. The reverse bears a Soldatenbrief stamp for Hus. Regt. 19 and a Feldpost stamp for 40. Infanterie-Division.

The duties of a Husar could vary greatly as seen in this photograph. Here a Husar wearing an M1910 attila with a marksman's lanyard, Husar breeches and boots with spurs, stands by his trusty steed, in this case, a bicycle. His companion, an NCO of an infantry regiment, has been awarded the Iron Cross 2nd Class as evidenced by the ribbon in his buttonhole. The reverse is Feldpost dated 27 September 1916 and a written message says "EinRadfahrer in Russland" (a bicyclist in Russia).

Trick photography was possible during World War I as we see a lonely Husar gefreiter dreaming of his wife at home. In this study our Husar wears an M1910 gray attila and breeches, a field service visor cap, and Husar boots. The date and the name of the enterprising studio are unknown.

A troop from Husaren-Regiment v. Zeiten (Brandenburgisches) Nr. 3 pose for Dörnitz photographer Voss in June of 1908. Hus. R. 3 wore red attilas with white cording and black sealskin Pelzmützen with red mützenbeutel bags. In the photograph most are wearing full equipment, but are not dressed for parade. M1889 cavalry swords, M1890 lances without pennants, and Kar 88.s are their weapons of the day.

This large family group has a decidedly military presence. An Ulan, two Husars, and an infantry officer make up the group. The occasion for the photo is unclear, but some are formally dressed while others seem to be dressed as domestics. One Husar wears his Pelzmütze with officer-style cap lines and with an unusual round feldabzeichen, plus a cold weather jacket called a pelz which also appears to have officers frogging. It would appear from the picture this man was serving in the Hus. R. 8 or Hus. R. 15. The second Husar is a senior NCO and wears a pre-war M1895 attila.

The men of 2. Leib-Husaren-Regiment Königin Viktoria von Preussen Nr. 2 gather to celebrate Christmas 1911. The Totenkopf, or death's head insignia worn by Leib-Husaren-Regiment Nr. 1 and Leib-Husaren Regiment Nr. 2, can be seen on both the Pelzmützen and the mützen caps. Their attilas and Husar breeches were black with white cording and the mützenbeutel, or bag, on the sealskin Pelzmützen was white. Close inspection of the shoulder straps shows the crown over "V" cypher unique to the regiment.

A formal photograph of an unidentified Husar regiment shows the men wearing M1895 attilas and dark Husar breeches and boots. The distinctive decoration on the boot tops is clearly shown, as are the M1889 cavalry swords. Mützen and visor caps in the regimental colors and piping were the headgear for the day. The reverse is dated 1912.

A Husar trooper in a full-length studio portrait taken somewhere in France. He is attired in the M1910 gray attila, Husar breeches and regimentally piped gray mütze. He is armed with an M1889 cavalry sword. An excellent study of a wartime Husar still on mounted service.

Uniforms and Equipment of the Imperial German Army 1900-1918

A wonderful studio portrait of a young Feldwebel from Husaren-Regiment v. Schill (1. Schlesisches) Nr. 4 wearing a private purchase M1910 attila and an M1910 officer grade visor cap. The eye patch covering a wounded eye gives him a Hollywood movie film appearance, but his valor is not in question as indicated by the ribbon of the Iron Cross 2nd Class worn on his attila.

Railroad - Eisenbahn Troops

A Bavarian Eisenbahn trooper wearing an unusual Bavarian M1916 Feldbluse with blue and white tape on the collar edges, litzen on the collars, and M15 colored shoulder straps bearing the script "E". He has been issued the billed cap for drivers, medics, and some mountain troops, plus leg-wraps and schnürschuh M1901 front-laced boots, and what appears to be an old Gew 71. Troops called Feldeisenbahn were assigned to the Macedonian Front, as well as to the Alpenkorps who fought at Verdun.

ABOVE: Recruits from the Bavarian Eisenbahn Batallion (Munich) pose for their photograph on 11 November 1914. One would wonder how many survived four years from that date. They wear a mixture of M1910 Bavarian tunics and M1895 dark blue uniforms with litzen, Shakos, visor caps, and blue, as well as gray, mützen. Armament consists of Gew 88.s and S98/05 bayonets. The reverse is Feldpost stamped and dated.

On the right is an Unteroffizier of the Bavarian Eisenbahn Batallion wearing a Bavarian M1910/15 tunic with rampant lion buttons, double litzen for technical troops, Iron Cross 2nd Class and Bavarian War Service ribbons and a script "E" on his shoulder straps. His companion has "1" on his shoulder straps which in all probability is for the 1st Bavarian Jäger Batallion. The photograph was taken in the Willy Watcher Studio in Munich and is dated 1917.

The Munich studio of Hermann Tietz took this photograph of five members of the Bavarian Eisenbahn Batallion on 10 November 1914. Four are wearing M1895 uniforms as issued to recruits and one wears an M1910 uniform with a field-covered shako and feldabziechen. The others wear mützen and Bavarian uncovered shakos. On the reverse the sender's rank is listed as "Pioneer" which was the title of a private in Bavarian Eisenbahn troops.

Concern is plainly marked on the face of the wife of this Prussian Eisenbahn soldier about to depart for the front. The script chain-stitched "E" for Eisenbahn can be seen on the shoulder straps of his M1910 uniform. His brass-trimmed pickelhaube has the field cover in place and his field equipment includes a Gew 88. The reverse is postmarked 16 January 1915.

A Bavarian Eisenbahn Batallion Pionier poses in an M1895 blue tunic, corduroy trousers and an ersatz feldgrau felt Bavarian shako for the Munich studio of Statchus. The date was late 1914.

Anti-Aircraft Artillery

RIGHT: This commercial postcard by Imberg and Lefson of Berlin shows the medium Flak range-finder, or Enterfernungamesser, in use on a tripod. A Flak battery can be seen in the background.

BELOW: Officers, NCOs and Kanoniers of Flak Artillerie Regiment Nr. 22 pose by an anti-aircraft gun emplacement somewhere in France. Everyone is dressed in their best for this occasion as can be seen by the polished boots and tidy pressed uniforms of the M1910, M1910/15 and M1915 variety. Mounted troop boots are seen, as well as spurs on the officers and NCOs. The reverse bears the date of July 1916.

A mobile-mounted Flak anti-aircraft gun motors down a tree-lined French road with two drivers in the front seat. This Krupp-Daimler combination was first introduced as a Zeppelin/Balloon defense gun using a modified 7.5 cm field gun and later in 1917-18, modified to accommodate an 8.8 cm gun, a caliber later used in World War II.

A lightweight automatic Flak gun and its four-man crew were photographed in August of 1916. The NCO observer is equipped with Zeiss binoculars superior to the issue Fernglas 08 and all wear M1910 uniforms. The gun was a one-pounder and was water-cooled.

An unusual photograph of a horse-drawn mast searchlight and its crew. The location was near the front as a wounded soldier and a medic stand in the rear center of the picture. To operate, the mast was set up in the vertical and the light could be pivoted in any direction. Used in anti-aircraft work with Flak batteries, but also used in the front lines to protect against trench raids. The reverse is dated 28 August 1916 and addressed to Karlsruhe.

This Flak battery was photographed in France at the end of May 1916. Interestingly, the crew of seven are wearing ball-topped pickelhauben with field covers, while the observers in the background wear mützen. One of the officers is calmly smoking a pipe, so it would seem this is a posed rather than action picture.

The crew in this and the following photograph were taken from various artillery units in the area as their shoulder straps bear different numbers and cyphers. Their uniforms are M1910, 1910/15 and M1915. They wear a variety of footwear from mounted boots to side-laced M1893 schnürschuh. Two fuse setters, a loader, a man at the firing lanyard, a man at the optical sight, a man working the elevation, another stationed by a drift sight and an NCO in charge make up the crew.

The same gun with a different and larger crew pose in these July 1916 photos. This crew has added another NCO and loader making a total of ten, which may be more than necessary when in action.

Air Service

A young pilot poses in his flying gear before an Albatros B or C type two-seater. He holds a flyer's Sturshelm M13 crash helmet in his right hand and wears a soft leather helmet and goggles, a long gray-knitted scarf and a plain leather 3/4 length coat.

An interesting photo of a group of NCOs undergoing aerial gunnery training with a modified Maxim Parabellum Aircraft Machine gun M1913. This modification by Karl Heinemann created the lightest Maxim ever designed, weighing only 22 pounds. Most are wearing M1910/15 tunics with Air Service shoulder straps with the winger propeller device.

The graves of Ltn. Eric Hagedorn, pilot, and Ltn. Friedrich Swoboda, observer from Flieger Abteilung 234. The date of their death was 4 June 1917. Note the broken propeller and memorial wreath.

A studio portrait of Leutnant Alfred Holz of Flieger Abteilung 253 in his M1910 tunic with Air Service shoulder straps. He had been awarded the Iron Cross 2nd Class and wears the Imperial Air Service Observer's badge.

An officer of the Saxon Karabinier-Rgt. (2. Schweres Rgt.) who had transferred into the Air Service retaining his original cavalry-style tunic with Air Service shoulder straps. The tunic is of a heavy twill material used during the war for field service uniforms.

During the war the firm of Postkartenvertrieb W. Sanke of Berlin produced a huge series of personality and hero photo postcards of which this and many to follow are examples. These cards, particularly those of flyers, are eagerly collected today. This is a view of Leutnant Hans Ritter von Adam who was killed in action 15 November 1917 flying an Albatros D V, having scored 21 victories. He was a Bavarian, wounded while serving with the infantry, joined the Air Service in 1916 as an observer, became a pilot in February 1917, and served with Jasta 34 and 6, of which he became Staffelfuhrer. He was awarded the Iron Cross 1st and 2nd Class, Bavarian Military Merit Order with swords, and posthumously, the Knights Cross with Swords of the Hohenzollern House Order on 2 February 1918.

Six pilots and observers pose in a winter setting before an Albatros C-type observation plane. The individuality of the Air Service personnel can be seen in the varied flying clothes worn in this photograph. They are all equipped with the Sturzhelm M13 crash helmets and three are holding altimeter recording devices.

Two captured English airmen after their interrogation at a divisional headquarters somewhere in France. The Mercedes staff car would take them on to a POW compound. The reverse states they were captured in 1915, but no other date.

Another Sanke card of Leutnant Hermann Pfeiffer, 11 victories, killed on 20 May 1917 while testing a captured Nieuport fighter. Originally he served with Bavarian Infantry Regiment 114, winning the Iron Cross 2nd Class in May 1915, and in July he entered pilot training. In July 1917 he was assigned to Armee Staffel AOK 3 flying single-seater Fokkers which later became Jasta 9. He was awarded the Iron Cross 1st Class, the Silver Military Karl-Friedrich Verdeinst Medal, and later he was commissioned and awarded the Militarischer Karl-Friedrich Verdeinst-Order.

Observer Oberleutnant Gerlich wearing his infantry shoulder straps on a modified M1915 bluse, the Iron Cross 1st Class and an observer's badge poses with his dog for Sanke card number 388.

Five NCO student pilots pose with their flight instructor in the white helmet and flying suit by a DFW Deutsche Flugzeugwerke C-type aircraft. A mechanic stands on the wing holding a flight instrument.

Mechanics and flight crews pose by an Albatros C-type armed with a Parabellum M13 machine gun in the rear cockpit. The photo is dated Belgium June 1918 on the reverse. It is interesting to note that as the war progressed, the use of crash helmets lessened and none are shown in this later war photograph.

The tallest and the shortest members of the 3rd Flieger Kompanie of a Garde detachment pose before the doors of a large hangar. The uniforms are of interest as the Garde litzen are on both collars, but only on the cuffs of the short man. They wear highly unusual feldgrau oilcloth caps with silver Garde star insignia and the chinstraps in the lowered position. They are armed with Kar 98a's and equipped with M1895 patronentaschen ammo pouches.

A seldom seen view of a member of the Württemberg Flieger Ersatz Abteilung Nr. 10 taken near the Boeblingen Airfield in 1915-16. Our man is wearing an extremely rare shako with a Württemberg feldabzeichen and gray-painted Garde star frontplate, an M1915 Feldbluse, collar litzen and winged propeller and numbered "10" shoulder straps.

Unteroffizier Alfred Friedrich of Garde Flieger Batallion Nr. 1 who was awarded both classes of the Iron Cross and a war service cross appears in Sanke card 394. He is wearing an M1910 tunic with Garde litzen, his Prussian pilot's badge, an open claw belt supporting a dress bayonet with portapee. Friedrich is not listed as being a fighter ace, but may have gained fame in another arm of the Air Service.

Ground personnel of Bavarian Flieger Abteilung Nr. 298 pose near their airfield with their pet rabbits at the end of March 1918. Two NCOs on the far right hold their rabbits in their visor caps, while the fourth from the right puts his stahlhelm to the same use. The reverse was signed Pion. Jos. Schorer F. A. 298, 27.3.18.

This group of Bavarian NCOs and officers were in flight training at the flying school near the Lechfeld lager when they posed for this photo by F. W. Putsch from the "Bavaria" Studio. All but two are wearing the fleece-lined, fur-collared flying overcoats over a variety of M1910/15 and M1915 uniforms. The Bavarian borte is in evidence on many of the collars of their uniforms, as are the ribbons for bravery awards.

Good uniform detail can be found in this formal portrait of a Prussian flying service NCO. The Flieger diamond pattern NCO tresse borders his collar, Officer double litzen collar tabs, M15 enlisted shoulder straps with the winged propeller device and the ribbon for the Iron Cross 2nd Class adorn his M15 Feldbluse with breast pocket flaps.

A Prussian NCO from Flieger Abteilung 27 poses for his photograph wearing a white shirt and necktie under his M1915 Feldbluse. The Abteilung numbers 27 appear on his left sleeve and shoulder straps, and his visor cap has that jaunty look so favored by aviators of all periods.

The Imperial Naval Air Service had their aces too, as was Oberflugmeister Karl Meyer. He shot down eight enemy aircraft including an airship on 21 April 1917 and was the first ace of the Naval Air Service. He died in Leipzig on 31 December 1917 of injuries sustained in a flying accident. In this photograph he wears the ribbon for the Iron Cross 2nd Class, the Iron Cross 1st Class and the Naval pilot's badge which bears an eagle in flight. Sanke card 411.

Sanke card 412 of another Naval airman. This portrait of Leutnant zur See Boenisch shows he was an observer as indicated by the badge below his Iron Cross depicting an eagle watching a setting sun. The particulars of Boenisch's career in Naval aviation are unknown to the author.

A Bavarian NCO stands for his picture in an M1895 Flieger unit dress uniform with winged propeller shoulder straps. His visor cap on the chair bears an Edelweiss badge on its side which is unusual, and he has been awarded the Iron Cross 2nd Class.

An enlisted man wearing an M1910/15 Flieger troops tunic and visor cap poses by a DFW C-type two-seater airplane. The reverse of the photo bears the caption "Fla 6 Grossenheim".

Uniforms and Equipment of the Imperial German Army 1900-1918

Carl Haug, photographer from Ingolstadt, captured these three Bavarian Luftschiffer troops wearing M1895 uniforms with script "L" on the shoulder straps, visor caps and M1893 schnürschuh side-laced boots.

BELOW: A fine photograph of the Luftschiff "L 3" taken against a leaden sky. Careful inspection of the lower right corner reveals the large ground crew who have just been involved in the "L 3s" departure from the field.

Rittmeister Prinz Friedrich Sigismund von Preussen is the subject of Sanke card 580. He is wearing a modified Husar uniform with the death's head insignia of Husar Regt. Nr. 2 on his visor cap, Iron Cross 2nd Class ribbon, Iron Cross 1st Class, his pilot's Abzeichen below the Iron Cross and winged propellers on his shoulder straps.

Leutnant Helmuth Hirth poses for the Sanke photographer wearing an M1910 tunic, the Iron Cross 2nd Class, pilot's Abzeichen, leather officers belt and dress bayonet. Ltn. Hirth's deeds of valor are unknown and he does not rank in the list of fighter aces. Possibly he had performed well in a bomber or observation squadron. Sanke card 7824.

Uniforms and Equipment of the Imperial German Army 1900-1918

An enlisted pilot from the Marineflieger Abteilung, as indicated on his cap tally, was photographed in a studio setting. The silver Abzeichen fur Marine-Flugzeugführer von Landflugzeugen can be plainly seen worn below his belt; above it, over the belt, is a bronze award which is not identified.

A photograph, which in all probability was taken near a flying school, of a pilot wearing a Fliegerkombination one-piece leather suit with a full fur collar, a long scarf in field gray and a leather helmet with goggles.

Leutnant Hartmut Baldamus, an 18 victory ace who flew with FFA (Feldflieger Abteilung) 20 and Jastas 5 and 9, is pictured in Sanke 432. He is seen here wearing an M1910 tunic and carrying an IOD 89 sword. His awards, before he was killed in a collision with a French Nieuport on 14 April 1917, included both classes of the Iron Cross, the Albert Order, Knight 2nd Class and the Knights Cross with Swords of the Hohenzollern House Order. He was two victories shy for the award of the Pour-le-Mérite when he died.

Oberleutnant Kurt Wolff, 33 victory ace of Jastas 11 and 29, strikes a Napoleon-like pose for Sanke card 513. He flew with von Richthofen in Jasta 11 and became commander of Jasta 29. He was awarded the Knights Cross with Swords of the Royal Hohenzollern House Order on 26 April 1917 and the Pour-le-Mérite on 4 May 1917. He was killed in action on 15 September 1917 by flight Sub Lt. N. M. McGregor flying a RNAS Camel.

A student pilot poses for his graduation photograph wearing heavy canvas flying coveralls and a leather helmet and goggles. He has Flieger litzen on the collar tabs of his feldgrau uniform seen under his flying clothing.

A finely-detailed studio photograph of a recently trained pilot. He is wearing the early war-style M13 crash helmet with goggles, a woolen scarf and a black leather flying coat with a fur collar and M1910 gray buttons. The style of the flying coat minus the fur collar is similar to those worn by the Kraftfaher motor vehicle drivers seen earlier in this volume.

Uniforms and Equipment of the Imperial German Army 1900-1918

A Prussian Feldwebel wearing a leather flying helmet and goggles, M1915 Feldbluse with Garde tresse and litzen on the collar, Feldwebel collar button, and Air Service shoulder straps sits for this formal studio portrait.

An offizierstellvertretter (an NCO with a wartime rank of junior Leutnant) has chosen an artistic style for his studio portrait. The shoulder straps are specific to his rank and bear the Air Service winged propeller device.

Sanke card 401 shows Vizefeldwebel, later Leutnant, Rudolf Windisch, 22 victories, on the right, and Oberleutnant Maximillian von Cossel his observer. Windisch and von Cossel were highly decorated for an unusual feat on the Russian Front. This involved landing behind Russian lines, dropping off von Cossel, who in turn blew up an important railway bridge near Rowno-Brody. The following day Windisch returned to the same site, picked up von Cossel and brought him back to FFA 62s airfield. The Kaiser personally awarded both men with the Prussian Crown Order 4th Class with Swords for this action. Windisch was shot down and presumed captured on 27 May 1918, but was never repatriated at the end of the war. There was a rumor he was shot and killed attempting escape and while stealing a French aircraft, but no proof has been made. Both men are wearing M1910 uniforms, with Windisch wearing a numbered patch indicating FFA 62.

A young student pilot sits for his formal graduation portrait wearing a gray-painted leather crash helmet with a balaklava-knitted wool cold weather helmet under it, goggles, long scarf, and flyers short overcoat. The reverse is dated 10 September 1918 which is late for the wearing of a M13 crash helmet.

A serious NCO Flieger poses for a studio photographer wearing a leather flying helmet, fur-edged goggles, a leather flying coat with a raccoon or fox fur collar and lining. The coat bears Prussian buttons and his tunic shows NCO flyers collar tresse and litzen.

Leutnant Max Ritter von Mulzer, first Bavarian ace, first Bavarian to be awarded the Pour-le-Mérite, and the first Bavarian knight receiving the Knights Cross of the Military Max-Joseph Order. He first served with 8 Chavaulegers-Regiment and is wearing that uniform in this Sanke card 385. He scored 10 victories in 1916 and was killed 26 September 1916 testing an Albatros D1.

Leutnant Karl Emil Schäfer, 30 victory ace, stands next to his Albatros DV in Sanke card 512. After his first victory with Jasta 11 of KG 3, he was assigned to von Richthofen's Jasta 11 and was given command of Jasta 28 on 26 April 1917. He was killed in action in combat with 20 Squadron RFC.

A casual pose is struck by this Bavarian Flieger wearing a leather flying helmet with goggles and a leather mid-weight fleece-lined flying coat which bears lion rampant Bavarian buttons on the front. The deep collar on this coat is interesting as it would have practically covered his face if turned up. He is wearing leg-wraps typical of flying personnel.

This airman wears another variety of leather flying coat. This model has civilian bone buttons, no shoulder straps, and copious pockets. His long gray-knitted scarf is worn in a prominent manner and it is interesting to note that his helmet is lined with rabbit fur.

Leutnant Johannes Klein, 16 victory ace with Jastas 29, 18, 15. He was awarded the Knights Cross with Swords of the Hohenzollern House Order, and 1st and 2nd Classes of the Iron Cross. Sanke.

Kampf-Flieger Oberleutnant Stefan Kirmaier commanded Jasta 2 after the death of Boelcke. He flew with FAA 203, KEK J as well as Jasta 2, scoring 11 victories. He was shot down and killed by 24 Squadron RAF on 22 November 1916, the same day it was announced he had been awarded the Knights Cross with Swords of the Hohenzollern House Order. Sanke card 445.

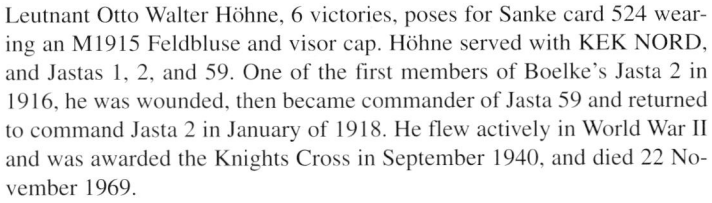

Leutnant Otto Walter Höhne, 6 victories, poses for Sanke card 524 wearing an M1915 Feldbluse and visor cap. Höhne served with KEK NORD, and Jastas 1, 2, and 59. One of the first members of Boelke's Jasta 2 in 1916, he was wounded, then became commander of Jasta 59 and returned to command Jasta 2 in January of 1918. He flew actively in World War II and was awarded the Knights Cross in September 1940, and died 22 November 1969.

Leutnant Walter Höhndorf, 12 victories, flew with Flieger-Abteilung 12 and 67, KEK VAUX, and Jastas 1, 4, 14. He was awarded the Pour-le-Mérite on 20 July 1916 and was killed in a flying accident 5 September 1917. He is pictured in Sanke card 381 wearing an M1915 bluse, the Iron Cross 1st Class, and the Pour-le-Mérite, dating the photograph after July 1916.

The Eagle of Lille, Oberleutnant Max Immelmann, 15 official victories, who flew with FFA 62 and KEK DOUAI. FFA 62 flew two-seaters, but had a section of Fokker Eindekkers which became KEK DOUAI. He and Oswald Boelke flew together, both becoming famous early fighter pilots. Max received his Pour-le-Mérite 12 January 1916, as well as earlier bestowals of the Iron Cross 1st Class, Knights Cross with Swords of the Hohenzollern House Order, Saxon Commander's Cross to the Military St. Henry Order 2nd Class, and the Knights Cross of this order, Saxon Albert Order 2nd Class with Swords, Saxon Friedrich-August Medal in Silver, Bavarian Military Merit Order 4th Class with swords, plus other lesser awards. He was killed in action 18 June 1916. He is pictured in Sanke card 362 with his dog and wearing his awards.

ABOVE: A group of Bavarian pilots photographed by F. W. Putsch at the airfield near Lechfeld. Ribbons for the Iron Cross 2nd Class are worn by two of the group and all but one are wearing the issued heavy gray wool flying coats, fleece-lined with fur collars.

A well-decorated Prussian Leutnant Beobachter observer is pictured wearing an M1910 tunic with officers Air Service shoulder boards, Iron Cross 1st Class, observers badge and ribbons for his other decorations.

Vizefeldwebel Friedrich Manschott of Jasta 7 achieved 12 victories from 15 December 1916 through 16 March 1917 when he was killed in a fight with four French Caudrons over Verdun. This was quite a record in only four months of combat and had he lived, he surely would have been one of the top scorers. Sanke card 449.

Leutnant Gustav Leffers who served with FFA 32 and KEK B which became Jasta 1, achieved 9 victories by 9 November 1916, four days after he was awarded the Pour-le-Mérite. He was also awarded the Knights Cross of the Hohenzollern House Order, two classes of the Oldenburg-Friedrich-August Cross and the Iron Cross 1st and 2nd Classes. On 27 December 1916 he was shot down and killed, possibly flying a captured Nieuport Scout which he was known to fly.

Hauptman Hans-Joachim Buddecke, 13 victories, flew with FA 23, Ottoman FA 6, Jasta 4, Ottoman FA 5, Jasta 30, and Jasta 18, and was shot down and killed on 10 March 1918.

Leutnant Walter von Bülow-Bothkamp, 28 victory ace, flew with FA 22 and 300, and Jastas 18, 36, and 2. He joined Braunschweig Husar-Rgt. Nr. 17 in 1914, and is seen in their uniform in Sanke card 582. He was awarded the Pour-le-Mérite on 8 October 1917, having already received the 1st and 2nd Class Iron Cross, the Knights Cross with Swords of the Hohenzollern House Order and the Saxon Military St. Henry Order. He was shot down and killed near Ypres by British fighters on 6 January 1918.

Tony Fokker is seated in Fokker DR I, Nr. 1729, General der Kavallerie von Hoeppner, Commander of the Air Service, rests his arm on the aircraft and next to him is Rittmeister Manfred Freiherr von Richthofen, 80 victories. The other two officers are unidentified.

Pilots and observers of Flieger-Abteilung 62 pose with a group of fighter aces. Identified in the front row, fourth from the left, is Hauptmann Oswald Boelke, 40 victories, killed in a collision 28 October 1916; next to him Hauptmann Kestner, CO of FA 62, and next to him, Oberleutnant Max Immelmann, 15 victories; back row far left, Leutnant Max Ritter von Mulzer, 10 victories, wearing his Chavauleger tunic and on the far right, an unidentified officer wearing a Husar tunic.

Hauptmann Adolf Ritter von Tutschek, 27 victories with FA 6, Jastas 2 and 12, and JG II. He was awarded the Iron Cross 1st and 2nd Classes, the Bavarian Military Merit Order 4th Class with Swords, the Military Max-Joseph Order, which gave him the title of Ritter, the Bavarian Military Merit Order with Crown and Swords, the Knights Cross with Swords of the Royal Hohenzollern House Order and on 3 August 1917, the Pour-le-Mérite. After scoring his 27th victory on 10 March 1918, he was shot down and killed flying his green Fokker DR I tri-plane near Brancourt by the British 24 Squadron.

Oberleutnant Max Immelmann was photographed standing by the wreckage of his seventh victim, a French Morane Parasol, brought down on 15 December 1915.

A Siemans Schuckert D. III A which many felt was the most superior German fighter built. With a 200 HP Siemans Halske engine, it climbed at a rate of 1,335 feet per minute, 500 feet per minute faster than the SPAD XIII C.I, the fastest Allied plane. This aircraft was introduced late in 1918.

Members of Feld-Flieger-Abteilung 19 enjoy a ride in the squadron staff car the winter of 1916-17. The staff car appears to be painted a light camouflage to blend into the snow in the background.

German ground personnel are pictured inspecting the remains of the British two-seater which was shot down 4 April 1916. The crew were reported to have been the pilot, Captain Thompson, and the observer, Captain Reid, both of whom were killed in the crash.

A smiling Rittmeister Manfred Freiherr von Richthofen and three unidentified officers were photographed at an airfield in Germany. The date of the picture is after 12 January 1917, which was the date of the award of his Pour-le-Mérite.

Hauptmann Eduard Ritter von Schleich, 35 victories, who flew with FA 2, SS 28, Jastas 21, 32, and Commander of Jagdgruppe Nr. 8 on the left was photographed with Oberleutnant Ernst Udet, 62 victories, the second highest ace who flew with FAA 206, FA 68, KEK H, and Jastas 15, 37, 11, 4. Hauptmann von Schleich was awarded his Pour-le-Mérite on 4 December 1917; Udet's award was in April of 1918, which in all probability dates this photo late spring or early summer 1918.

Jagdstaffel 6. Left to right: Leutnant Julius Schmidt, 15 victories, transferred to Jasta 6 on 9 September 1918; Leutnant Ulrich Neckel, 30 victories, was awarded the next to last Pour-le-Mérite 8 November, 1918; Leutnant Werner Näldecke, one victory; Leutnant Matzdorf, 2 victories; and Leutnant Schlieven, a non-flying officer. Of interest is the flying suit and parachute harness worn by Leutnant Matzdorf.

A wonderful view of an unidentified squadron which was equipped with a Fokker E IV, 5 Fokker D IIIs, an Albatros C Type, and 2 Fokker DIs. This photograph shows that when a Jasta was re-equipped with newer aircraft, it was by no means a total update and the older machines stayed in service.

Leutnant Nöchel, observer, and Leutnant Riezler, pilot, pose by their L.V.G.-C2 number 798. The Parabellum machine gun is clearly seen pointing aft from the rear cockpit. It is interesting to note how often the observer is wearing polished high leather boots and the pilot is in leg-wraps.

Offizierstellvertreter Otto Esswein, 12 victories, flying with Jasta 26, stands by his Fokker DR I in the spring of 1918. Esswein was killed in aerial combat on 21 July 1918, five days after successfully bailing out of his crippled Albatros DVa. Before his death, he won both classes of the Iron Cross, Golden Military Mérite Cross, and the Württemberg Military Medal in Gold and Silver.

An unidentified pilot wearing an Air Service fur-collared, fleece-lined flying coat and sporting a cane, stands by his Albatros D III which carries the personal marking "KP".

Leutnant Wilhelm Fahlbusch, 5 victories, flew Roland C II two-seaters scoring his victories early in 1916. He was shot down and killed by members of 70 Squadron RFC on 6 September 1916.

Leutnant Wilhelm Frankl, 20 victories, flying with FA 40 as an observer, KEK VAUX and Jasta 4. He was awarded the Iron Cross 1st Class for shooting an enemy aircraft with a carbine. He transferred to pilot training and later flew single-seat Fokker Eindekkers. 16 May 1916 he was promoted to Leutnant and days later was awarded the Knights Cross of the Hohenzollern House Order and the Pour-le-Mérite on 12 July 1916. He was killed in action on 8 April 1917 and is the only flyer of Jewish heritage to have a modern Luftwaffe fighter squadron, Nr. 74, to bear his name.

Leutnant Albert Dossenbach, 15 victories with FA 22 and Jastas 36 and 10. A former medical student, he enlisted in the Army in 1914, and received the Iron Cross 2nd and 1st Class for carrying his wounded CO to safety. Later, he received the Military Merit Cross and was commissioned in January 1915. He transferred to aviation and flew two-seaters with FA 22, scoring 8 victories with them. He was awarded the Knights Cross 2nd Class with Swords of the Order of the Zahringer Lion and the Knights Cross of the Hohenzollern House Order. 11 November 1916 he became the first two-seater pilot to receive the Pour-le-Mérite, which was soon followed by the Knights Cross of the Karl Friedrich Military Merit Order. He was killed in action on 3 July 1917 in a fight with four members of British 57 Squadron. Sanke card 416.

Another photo of Dossenbach posing by an Albatros C-type two-seater of the type in which he scored his first 9 victories. This is not a Sanke produced card.

Unser erfolgreicher Kampf-Flieger Oberleutnant Berthold.

Hauptman Rudolf Berthold, 44 victories with KEK VAUX, Jastas 4, 14, 18, and JG II. He suffered many wounds and injuries, but survived the war, only to be strangled by post-war rioters on 15 March 1920. He flew Pfalz E IVs and D IIIs, and later Fokker D VIIs. The personal markings were a white winged sword on a red and blue fuselage. He was awarded the Iron Cross 1st and 2nd Class, Bayerisch Kriegverdeinst-Order IV Class, the Ritterkrenz of the St. Heinrichs Order, the Knights Cross with Swords of the Hohenzollern House Order, on 12 October 1917, the Pour-le-Mérite, as well as the Saxon Knights Cross of the Military St. Henry Order. In Sanke card 402 he looks every part the nobleman Prussian pilot as depicted by Hollywood films.

Leutnant Joachim von Bertrab, 5 victories with Jasta 30. On 6 April 1917 while flying his black or purple Albatros D III with a comet design and white crosses edged in black, he downed four British bombers in two engagements. On 12 August 1917 he was shot down and captured by Lt. Edward "Mick" Mannock of 40 Squadron while attacking a balloon. Sanke card 530.

Oberleutnant Hans Berr, 10 victories scored with KEK AVILLERS and Jasta 5. Berr flew Fokker Eindekkers with KEK A, scoring twice. From this group Jasta 5 was formed, which he commanded. He was killed in action on 6 April 1917 after being awarded the Iron Cross 1st and 2nd Class, Knights Cross and Swords of the Hohenzollern House Order and the Pour-le-Mérite on 4 December 1916. He was also awarded the Bavarian Merit Order 4th Class with Swords, the Ruess War Merit Cross and Honor Cross 3rd Class with Swords, the Brunswick War Merit Cross 2nd Class and the Hanseatic Cross from Hamburg. Sanke card 425.

Oberleutnant Fritz Otto Bernert 27 victory ace who flew with FFA 27 and 71, KEK VAUX, and Jastas 4, 2, and 6. He served with Infanterie Regiment Nr. 173 and was wounded four times including a bayonet wound which severed the nerve in his left arm. Being unfit for Army duty, he joined the Air Service and flew skillfully with only one good arm. He was awarded the Iron Cross 1st and 2nd Class, the Saxon Albert Order, Knight 2nd Class with Swords, the Knights Cross with Swords of the Hohenzollern House Order and on 23 April 1917, the Pour-le-Mérite. To prove his worth, the next day he shot down a record five enemy aircraft in one action. He died of influenza on 18 October 1918.

BELOW: The sad end for two airmen, a fate met by so many from both sides. One of these victims was an officer who was in all probability the observer, the other the enlisted pilot. The two crash helmets would indicate a mid-war photo date for this tragedy.

Commissary

The kitchen detachment of Minenwerfer-Komp 309 pose by their stoves hidden under a camouflaged shelter. The sanitary conditions leave a little to be desired. Proceeds from the sale of this card went to an aid fund of the 25th Reserve Division.

On the reverse of this card is written "Sunday morning in reserve". The photo shows a group of five enjoying some liquid refreshment and wearing a mixture of M1910 uniforms and cotton shirts.

This photograph of a field bakery was taken in Russia, July 1916. The dough making and the forming of the loaves of bread is done in the tents on the right and then put into the field ovens on the left. A Landsturm guard, a decorated NCO and a young colt can be seen in the foreground and a Russian church in the right background.

A good view of a portable field stove and limber is seen in this photograph. The six-man crew are surrounded by an assortment of large pots and pails, as well as other instruments of their culinary trade. Two are wearing M1910/15 tunics which places the date as late as 1915 or early 1916.

Two portable field kitchens and commissary wagons are set up in a pine grove for cover from enemy observation. The man on the right seems to be staring intently at the contents of one large cauldron with a raised cover.

K. P. duty was performed and overseen by a member of Prussian Infanterie Regiment Nr. 17 on 22 June 1915. The striped pajamas and slipper outfits would make one think that these men are recuperating in a hospital.

The Feldpost stamped on the reverse of this photo card is for Maschine Gewehr Kompanie I of Infantry Regiment Nr. 151, dated 13 June 1917. The portable field stove, limber and horses are all visible, as are various other implements necessary for the preparation of food. Of particular interest is the seated medic on the right, as well as the huge bottle at the lower right.

A celebration, possibly a birthday, is in progress as seen in this photograph. On the table a stereo view of a woman in a white hat can be seen along with opened and unopened parcels, mess tins, and aluminum cups. The man in full uniform is prepared to serve something hidden behind the flowers. Letters and fresh loaves of bread complete the array of props on the table.

Uniforms and Equipment of the Imperial German Army 1900-1918

The reverse of this somewhat faded photograph is officially stamped "Koenigl.Preussische reserve-Sanitäts Komp No. 3. In the picture we see Sanitary Korps men wearing visor caps, Red Cross arm bands, M1910 tunics and fatigue uniforms. Food pails are suspended on a pole over a fire on the right, but the most unusual feature in the picture is the large head of a pig in front of the man seated on the left. There are no clues as to its significance.

Another faded, but interesting photo of a company of infantry lining up by their portable field kitchen for an evening meal, the time indicated by the long shadows. The man on the left holding his canteen, has been awarded the Iron Cross 2nd Class; the man third from the left is a drummer, as his drumsticks holder and drum suspension hanger are on his belt. M1910 uniforms are worn and those who are armed carry Gew 98.s and their patronentaschen suspended by breadbag straps. Many of the men are carrying large mess tins, possibly to carry food back to those in the trenches.

Chickens and rabbits are both being tended by an NCO and his assistants in this pastoral photograph. An interesting note is the barbed wire above the fence which was not intended to keep the animals in, but rather to keep foraging soldiers out.

Members of 7. Batterie-Bay. Res-Feldart. Regt. 9 take time from their gunnery duties to play cards, smoke, and enjoy some unidentified beverages. The card is dated by the sender, 19 August 1918.

The reverse of this photograph is dated 12 July 1915 and Feldpost stamped "San. Kraftw. Kol. D.6. Armee". The caps worn by the two men on the right are of the style worn by sanitary or medical troops and the man in the center with the briefcase is a Red Cross official. The future of the two large hogs does not look too bright from the looks of the large sledge hammer and the butcher's apron of the man in the lower right.

The stock of the canteens of the 4th Batallion, 167 Infantry Regiment, 22 Infantry Division is on display in this photograph mailed 10 November 1916. Two of the group have been awarded the Iron Cross 2nd class and a mixture of M1910, 1910/15, and fatigue uniforms are worn. Several men seem to be involved in inventory taking and a supply wagon and a Russian farmhouse are in the background.

Uniforms and Equipment of the Imperial German Army 1900-1918

From the black bands visible on the mützen and visor caps seen in this photo, the group are from an artillery, or minenwerfer, unit. Many Iron Cross 2nd Class ribbons are worn by those dressed in 1910/15 tunics, indicating a combat unit. The presence of the two sturdy cows and the well-fed hog are interesting and must have some bearing on the feeding of the unit.

This photo taken in October 1915 shows the butchers and their wares at the Military Rations Establishment at Chambley in Northern France. The hanging meat is pork. The quaint weathervane on the building is dated 1915.

Away from the front, this domestically inclined group are relaxed with their pipes, cigars, and a coffee grinder. A tub of potatoes and a loaf of bread can be seen with mess kits, canteens and cups on the table. M1910 and 1910/15 tunics are worn and cyphered and numbered shoulder straps are in evidence, but the unit cannot be identified. The reverse is dated 11 December 1915.

This field kitchen, limber, and staff are leaving for the front as indicated by the floral display worn by all of these Landsturm troops. They wear 1910 tunics; the three on the left are NCOs, and of particular interest are the cloth field covers on the oilskin landwehr caps of the dismounted men.

Uniforms and Equipment of the Imperial German Army 1900-1918

The reverse of this photo card bears the date of 1 November 1918 and a Brief-stempel of the 3rd Company of Landsturm Infanterie Regiment No. 13. The man on the right has the number 24 and Roman numeral XIII on the collar of his M1915 bluse. These two Landsturmers have been on a foraging party and are returning with a handsome fish and a brace of ducks. Food in 1918 was scarce, so these additions to the mess must have been most welcome.

Heavy Artillery

The four photographs that follow are of the same railroad gun taken at different locations with different crews. The gun was mounted on a special railcar with the serial number 602938 appearing in each photo. This view, taken in the winter with snow on the ground, was taken by the Robert Franck Studio in Düsseldorf, and in all probability, was taken soon after the gun's manufacture. Thirty-eight men pose in the picture.

This photo was taken in late spring with a crew of 41, plus a sentry. It is interesting to note that a four-part wicker screen has been mounted on the railcar below the elevated barrel and the inclusion of two small children in the picture on the right would indicate that a village is not far away.

The weather was still cold when this view was taken, as many of the crew are wearing overcoats and other M1910/15 uniforms. The forty-seven men seen here are indeed posing, but it is interesting to see a large projectile on a hoist being moved toward the breech. Two of the wicker screens are in place under the barrel, but it is still uncertain as to their function.

This crew was seen in an earlier view and wear an assortment of M1910/15 tunics and M1915 bluses, and a variety of footwear. They have changed their positions on the rail gun and two new young visitors are on the right. It is unfortunate that more information is not at hand on this interesting piece of heavy artillery.

A Naval 17 cm field gun in position on the coast of France in 1917. This camouflaged gun further utilizes netting to hide its outline. A study of the uniforms pictured here shows a diversity of Naval garb from the sailor's work blouse with collar, M1910/15 tunics, M1915 bluse, blue Naval reefer jacket and variations of fatigue uniforms and caps.

Three steam traction engines are employed in moving heavy artillery pieces and the attendant equipment wagons, as shown in this photograph taken somewhere in France. The cannon in the foreground appears to be a 17 cm gun with a temporary box-like wooden shield in place, and the personnel are artillerymen wearing a mixture of fatigue and M1910 tunics, ball-topped pickelhauben with field covers, mützen and visor caps with the black artillery bands.

A long-range, long-barrelled gun in a wooded emplacement points toward enemy lines. Manufactured by Krupp, this gun hurled a 15 cm shell for many miles. An example of the projectile can be seen standing near the breech.

Similar to the preceding gun, this long-range 15 cm piece is mounted on a double recoil rail track to compensate for the enormous force created by its firing. The loader's platform is seen by the breech, and the aiming and elevation crew have a platform by the gun trunions.

Camouflage netting protects this Krupp 17 cm medium range gun from observation from the air, while the gun itself retains the factory gray paint, rather than the camouflage tortoise pattern paint often seen. A partial crew poses with the gun wearing a mix of M1910/15, M15 and fatigue uniforms. Note the canvas breech cover for protection against the weather.

An interesting photograph of a 15 cm long-range gun being hauled to the front by a steam traction engine. Most movement of heavy artillery pieces was performed by these steam-driven tractors which were modified from civilian use to military. An officer on horseback stands behind the gun; he and the other men on foot are wearing M1910/15 uniforms.

This long (lange)-barreled 15 cm Howitzer is set in firing position in the ruins of a French farm. The wheels are carrying the large flat treads for traversing soft ground and heavy woven mats are in place under the gun. The crew wear M1910 tunics, fatigue jackets, and mützen with black artillery bands. The reverse of the photo is dated 13 August 1915.

This M1916 long-range 15 cm Krupp gun was photographed in a French village square in the spring of 1918. The lozenge pattern camouflage paint on the cannon is similar in style to that used on German aircraft. Twenty-one men surround the piece, officers and men, wearing a mixture of overcoats, M15 bluse, and M1910/15 uniforms. The reverse is dated from the field 29 May 1918.

ABOVE: Die dicke Berta (Big Bertha) officially known as M-Gerät L/12 is shown in this photograph taken by the studio of Karl Knauff of Mörs. The 42 cm Howitzer appears to be factory fresh and its accessories, sponge rammer, loading crane, and huge projectiles are clearly seen. The man on the right shows, by comparison, how huge this gun actually was.

An artilleryman wearing the M1895 blue uniforms poses by the breech of a 150 mm cannon mounted for fortress defense. The steel wheel at the base of the gun allows it to be traversed within its stone emplacement. The reverse is dated 1915.

Horses and Pets

Wearing the ribbons of the Iron Cross 2nd Class, a group of combat medics pose with their pet cats at Totaru on the Eastern Front, the summer of 1918. A mixture of M1910, M1910/15 and fatigue uniforms are worn and white Red Cross brassards are in evidence on the arms of two of the men.

A pleasant view of a decorated officer, his horse, and by his feet, a small dog which was moving when the photo was taken. He wears an M1910 tunic, a visor cap with a chinstrap, the Iron Cross 1st Class, the ribbon for the Iron Cross 2nd Class, leather dress gloves and a riding crop. The tack and saddlery on the horse are clearly shown.

Uniforms and Equipment of the Imperial German Army 1900-1918

The inclusion of the pet dog, or mascot, held by an NCO gives a human touch to this occupational photograph. The men are part of a construction crew posing at their various tasks. The second from the left has been planing boards as seen by the pile of shavings, a bow saw is in use, a mason's trowel is held by the central figure with suspenders, two men hold a paint, or whitewash, spraying device, and the man with the pipe holds a paintbrush at the ready.

Another occupational view shows five farriers at their work horseshoeing a dappled gray team horse. The photograph bears two dates, on the front 8 July 1918 and on the reverse 12 September 1918. The location was Arensburg Oesel. The sign over the door reads "Forge II Darmstadt".

The Brief-stempel mark on the reverse of this photo of a mounted artillery NCO reveals he was a member of Reserve-Fuss-Artl. Regt. 14, 2nd Batalion 3 Batterie. The Feldpost stamp indicates 8. Ersatz-Div. and the date 18 May 1915. He is wearing an M1910 uniform and is armed with a mounted artillery saber M1874.

These two pet goats make a welcome contribution to the food supply of this unidentified unit. A milk pail and pitcher are held by two eager milkers, while the third man from the left holds a cat who looks eager for its share. The majority of those in this photograph are wearing fatigue uniforms, but a few M1910/15 tunics can be seen.

A young infantryman and his faithful dog serving on the Flanders Front in 1917 dreams of his wife and child at home. These sentimental composite cards were quite popular as the war wore on. Our subject wears an M1915 bluse with the shoulder straps of a numbered regiment.

An officer and his "pony' pose for their photo somewhere in France. Our subject is wearing an M15 bluse and instead of riding boots, he has chosen Ledergamsche of the new model of 1914 and thick-soled schnüschuh-laced boots and spurs. The horse carries a large "H" branded on his flank, but no unit number can be seen. The "H" could possibly identify the horse as "Heer", or Army property.

Uniforms and Equipment of the Imperial German Army 1900-1918

A Prussian officer sits proudly astride his horse, with a frisky dog between the horse's legs. Dressed in his Uberrock, M1871/95 pickelhaube with the chinscales under the chin and armed with an IOD 89, he is the personification of the pre-war infantry officer. The reverse is dated 31 August 1905.

A group of NCOs enjoying a glass of wine is joined by a dachshund in the lap of the first seated man on the right of the table. The slight man on the front left is from Infanterie Regiment Nr. 113, a Baden regiment, but the numbers on the other shoulder straps are not legible. The word "unterstand" in military usage means "dug-out".

A well-groomed horse with a docked tail is the mount of choice of this well-bred appearing young officer. The photograph was taken by the studio of Anstalt L. Giesecke in Erlangen, Bavaria, and the date on the reverse is 8 October 1913.

What appears to be an orderly stands holding his officer's horse in this somewhat faded photograph. The man is wearing an M1910 uniform and mütze and generally looks well turned out.

ABOVE: A humorous photo taken in October, 1912 shows a wonderful variety of subjects and uniforms. The goat and cart overladen with beer kegs and people lends its own touch to the scene, while the beer drinking troops give a festive air. The mixture of M1895 uniforms, litewken, both for enlisted and NCOs, plus a drum and three Gew 98.s adds to the interest in this picture.

A young aristocratic officer complete with dueling scars poses with a gentle appearing horse in this unusual photograph. From the background, one would imagine the location was a permanent Kaserne in Germany.

Pickelhauben In Detail

The Berlin studio of A. Wertheim took this fine full-length portrait of a Leutnant in Prussian Infanterie Regiment 150. He wears his officer's grade pickelhaube with a Prussian line eagle frontplate, an M1910 uniform with "150" on the officer's shoulder straps, the Iron Cross 2nd Class, a brocade officer's dress belt, ledergamasche M1914 with laced shoes and carries a Prussian IOD M1889 sword with officer's sword knot.

It was the photographer Carl Zisch of the Munich studio of Stachus who captured this enlisted man of Bavarian Infanterie Regiment Nr. 2. His regiment is indicated by the crown and cyphered "MF" on the shoulder straps of his M1910 tunic. The Bavarian helmet plate and leather chinstrap can be seen on his pickelhaube and an S98 bayonet is held in his lap.

The rank of Offizierstellvertetter was an unusual one and in this portrait we see a man of that rank in a formal setting. Although he is not truly an officer, he wears an officer grade pickelhaube, M1910 tunic, and an officer grade "dove-head" sword. NCO collar decorations are in evidence, as are the special shoulder straps of his rank.

Prussian Leutnant Linden and his wife Agnes were photographed in Cöln-Nippes on 18 July 1915 soon after his return from the front. Linden, a Garde officer, wears his officer grade pickelhaube with the Garde Eagle and star, an M1910 tunic with Garde collar litzen, a brocade belt, or Feldbinde, and carries an IOD 89 sword with portapee.

An early war period photograph of a Saxon Infantryman and his wife in a studio setting. The Saxon helmet plate is clearly evident on his pickelhaube, as is his new M1910 uniform and 1901 stiefel, or marching boots. He is armed with a Gew 98. and an S98 bayonet.

An unusual photo of a Bavarian Infantryman wearing a brass-trimmed pickelhaube with a nicely detailed Bavarian helmet plate and a Prussian M1915 Feldbluse with Bavarian blue and white borte, or collar tape. The reverse is dated 3 June 1915, although the Bavarian issue Feldbluse was not officially introduced until 1916.

A Saxon reservist is photographed in a pickelhaube bearing a large reserve cross under the Saxon state coat of arms. This in an unusual and rarely seen helmet plate. Our man is equipped with an M1910 uniform, tornister 1895 pack, patronentaschen 1895, entrenching tool, or Schanzzeug 1887, and is armed with a Gew 98. with an S98 bayonet. The photo was by the Hugo Bartel studio in Leipzig and dated 19 October 1914.

A rather somber Württemberger poses on his wedding day with his smiling bride. He is from Württemberg Infanterie Regiment Nr. 246 as shown on the shoulder straps of his M1910 uniform and is holding his M1915 pickelhaube bearing the Württemberg helmet plate in gray. The photograph was taken by the Julius Berthold Studio in Feuerback (Stuttgart).

Atelier Scharrmann in Friedenau was the wedding photographer for this young Bavarian couple. The groom, an NCO, holds his M1915 gray-trimmed pickelhaube with the Bavarian frontal plate and wears the Bavarian-style M16 bluse with a Gefreiter rank button on the collar, as well as Bavarian borte on the collar edges. He has been awarded the Bavarian War Service Cross with Swords, which he proudly wears in this formal portrait.

Photographs of Hessian pickelhauben are not common; therefore, this clear view of an M1895 Hessian helmet is most welcome. The rampant Hessian lion plate can be easily recognized as are the man's M1910/15 tunic and ersatz bayonet. Karl Bethke studio in Darmstadt took the picture which is dated 4 November 1915.

This full-length study of a soldier from the 21st Bavarian Landsturm Infantry Company of the 1st Bavarian Army Corps is full of detail. He wears an M1915 gray-trimmed pickelhaube with a Bavarian frontplate, a Bavarian-style M1910/15 tunic with the unit designation metal collar insignia "I B" and "21", and corduroy combat trousers. His patronentasche are M1909, his Stiefel, or boots, M1906, and he is armed with a Gew 88., plus a silver-topped pipe in his right hand. The reverse is dated 10 July 1916.

Uniforms and Equipment of the Imperial German Army 1900-1918

A Prussian infantryman poses with his M1915 gray-trimmed pickelhaube with a Prussian-style frontplate wearing an M1915 bluse and field equipment. He is armed with a Gew 98.

This portrait was taken in 1914 of a young Bavarian private from Bavarian Infanterie Regiment Nr. 20. His pickelhaube is the model of 1895, trimmed in polished brass and bears the Bavarian frontplate. The balance of his uniform and equipment are classic early war as issued to front-line regular infantry regiments.

The wingspan of the Prussian eagle frontplate attached to the pickelhauben of Grenadier regiments was much wider than that supplied to line units. This can be seen in this photograph taken of a young Grenadier in full equipment taken in Döberitz on 3 October 1914. The pickelhaube is an M1895 with brass-scaled chinstraps, the binoculars are private purchase and his weapon a Gew 98.

The fluted spike, square-cut visor, flat-scaled chinstraps and Bavarian frontplate can be clearly seen in this 1916 dated picture of a Bavarian Landsturmer. The collar of his M1910 tunic bears "I B 18", which identifies him as a member of the First Bavarian Army Corps, Landsturm Infantry Batallion Nr. 18.

This photograph was taken in the second month of the war and gives an excellent view of the appearance of two fully-equipped Baden infantrymen. They are wearing the M1895 pickelhauben with brass trim, the winged Baden-griffin frontplates and leather chinstraps and M1910 uniforms and are armed with the Gew 98. complete with S98 quillback bayonets. The reverse carries a Brief-stempel for Baden Reserve Infantry Regiment 239 and the date 20 September 1914.

Füsiler Regiment Nrs. 33 and 34 wore a special frontplate on their pickelhauben which included a special band superimposed over the eagle, with an inscription commemorating distinguished service to the Swedes, an example of which is seen in this photograph. Our subject is a recruit to Füsiler Regiment Nr. 34 (Königin Viktoria von Schweden) and wears the regimental pickelhaube and an M1895 blue uniform as issued to recruits during training. The reverse is postmarked Stettin (the garrison town for the 34th), 29 December 1914.

Two recruits from Füsilier-Regiment Kaiser Franz Josef von Österrich, König von Ungarn, (4. Württembergisches) Nr. 122 pose wearing brass-trimmed pickelhauben displaying the Württemberg frontplate and leather chinstraps. They both wear M1895 uniforms, standard for early war recruits. The photograph was taken in the studio of L. Trinkner in Heilbronn, the garrison city for I. R. Nr. 122.

A Bavarian infantryman is photographed in the field with a portable backdrop with a grass-matting underfoot. His pickelhaube is an M1895 brass-trimmed with a Bavarian frontplate, and the leather chinstrap seems unusual as only one adjustment buckle can be seen. He wears an M1910 uniform, M1895 patronentaschen suspended in the combat-style by the breadbag strap and is armed with a Gew 88. and an S71 brass-hilted bayonet.

These two young Bavarians are about to depart for the front and pose wearing their M1895 brass-trimmed pickelhauben, M1910 uniforms, full field equipment, and Gew 98. rifles with S98/05 bayonets. An interesting detail is the use, by the man on the right, of his breadbag strap to support the patronentaschen, rather than the support strap of his tornister, or pack.

As the war progressed, brass became scarce and the M1915 pickelhaube as seen here was fitted with gray-painted steel instead of brass. In this portrait done by the H. Cordes Studio in Hildesheim, the subject is prepared to depart for the front as indicated by the flowers tucked into his M1910 tunic. Hildesheim was the garrison city of Infantry Regiment Nr. 79, so in all probability, he is from that regiment.

This Saxon infantryman is wearing an M1895 brass-trimmed pickelhaube with the Saxon frontplate and leather chinstrap. The shoulder straps on his M1910 tunic are numbered for 2. Grenadier-Regiment- Nr. 101 Kaiser Wilhelm, König von Preussen of XII Armee Korps. He carries a Gew 98. and an S98 bayonet with the M1895 patronentaschen.

Baden Leib-Grenadier Regiment Nr. 109 had a unique helmet plate which is seen in this photograph of an NCO from that regiment. The plate consisted of a standard Baden griffin-style, with a Garde star and cross superimposed. Our Grenadier wears an M1910 tunic with Grenadier litzen and carries a Gew 98. The photographer was Samson and Co., Karlsruhe, the garrison city of 1. Badisches Leib-Grenadier-Regiment Nr. 109.

Three Württemberg infantrymen are photographed wearing M1915 gray-trimmed pickelhauben with Württemberg frontplates and the M1915 Feldbluse. They are all armed with Gew 98. rifles and carry a mixture of M1909 and M1895 patronentaschen ammo boxes.

The widespread wings of the eagle on this M1895 brass-trimmed helmet identify it as belonging to a Grenadier regiment, five of which wore this same plate without additional battle honors. Our grenadier wears a rather unpressed M1910 uniform and full marching equipment.

A pickelhaube not often portrayed is this example of brass-trimmed M1895 from Mecklenberg-Strelitz. The regiment is the Grossherzoglich Mecklenburgisches Grenadier-Regiment Nr. 89 which was one of the ten regiments making the IX. Armeekorps. Our Grenadier is dressed in an M1910 uniform, and is armed with a Gew 88. The photograph was taken by Carl Wolff of Neustrelitz, the garrison town for Grenadier Regiment Nr. 89 and the reverse is dated 20 September 1914.

The Prussian line eagle plate on this M1895 pickelhaube bears a small silver reserve cross on the chest of the eagle, identifying this man as a member of the reserve. He wears a rather spotted M1894 overcoat and carries a small automatic pistol and an S98 bayonet on his service belt.

ABOVE: Not pickelhauben, but these mitre helmets which date back to the model of 1843 are of great rarity and interest. Presented to the III Batallion of the Kaiser Alexander Garde-Grenadier-Regiment Nr. 1 in 1894, these helmets were worn on ceremonial occasions only. This photograph shows Grenadiers in winter dress uniforms with white belts, Gew 98. rifles and M1895 patronentashcen. The reverse is dated Berlin, 18 March 1913.

This commercial photo-postcard portrays the national sentiment of Germany in November of 1914. The perfect reproduction of the M1895 pickelhaube, M1910 uniform and officers belt and buckle is evident in this patriotic and propaganda slanted photograph.

Chapter Two

Color Section

The color plates in this volume are reproduced from the original 93 Zeichnungen (illustrations) by Paul Casberg which were published by Verlag von Moritz Ruhl in Leipzig, 1916, in the volume entitled *Die Deutsche Armee in ihren neuen Feld-und Friedens-uniformen*. Starting in the 19th century, Ruhl published a quantity of uniform booklets which featured folding color plates depicting, both schematically and by figures, uniforms of the world. Books featuring flags, national and state heraldry, as well as poster-sized color sheets (43x59 cm) of uniform details were also published by the firm. An example of the large format style appears in the first Volume of this work and was entitled *Die grauen Felduniform der deutschen Armee 1914*.

Left to right: **Generalfeldmarschall** in der Bluse; **General der Infanterie** in der Bluse für Generale; **General der Artillerie** in Bluse und Stiefelhose (bei Frontdienst im Felde); **Vortragender Generaladjutant S.M. des Kaisers** in Bluse.

Left to right: **Flügeladjutant S.M. des Kaisers** im Waffenrock; **Major im Großen Generalstabe** in Bluse; **Hauptmann im Kriegsministerium** im Waffenrock.

Left to right: **1. Garde-Regiment zu Fuss**. Oberst im Waffenrock; **2. Garde-Regiment zu Fuss**. Major in Bluse; **3. Garde-Regiment zu Fuss**. Hauptmann im kleinen Rock; **4. Garde-Regiment zu Fuss**. Oberleutnant im Waffenrock.

Left to right: **Garde-Grenadier-Rgt. Nr. 5**. Feldwebel in Bluse; **K. Alexander-Garde-Grenadier-Regt. Nr. 1**. Unteroffizier im Mantel; **Königin Augusta-Garde-Grenadier-Regt. Nr. 4**. Grenadier im Waffenrock; **K. Franz-Garde-Grenadier-Regt. Nr. 2**. Grenadier in Bluse.

Left to right: **Leib-Grenadier-Regt. K.Friedr.Wilh.III. (1.Brand.) Nr. 8**. Hauptmann im kleinen Rock; **Grenadier-Regt. K. Wilhelm I. (2.Westpr.) Nr. 7**. Leutnant in Bluse; **Meckl. Grenadier-Regt. Nr. 89, II.Bat**. Leutnant im Mantel; **K.Sächs 2.Grenadier-Regt. Nr. 101 Kaiser Wilhelm**. Leutnant im Waffenrock.

Left to right: **1.Bad. Leib-Grenadier-Regt. Nr. 109**. Hauptmann im Waffenrock; **Bayer-Infanterie-Leib-Regt**. Oberleutnant in Bluse; **Leib-Garde-Infant.-Regt. (I.Gr.Hess.) Nr. 115**. Unteroffizier in Bluse; **Meckl. Grenadier-Regt. Nr. 89 I.u.III.Bat**. Grenadier in Bluse.

Left to right: **Füsilier-Regt. v. Gersdorff (Kurhess.) Nr. 80**. Hauptmann in Bluse; **Oldenb. Infanterie-Regt. Nr. 91**. Adjutant im Waffenrock; **Garde-Schützen-Bataillon**. Hauptmann im Waffenrock.

Left to right: **Infanterie-Regt. Graf Barfuß (4. Westfäl.) Nr. 17**. Unteroffizier im Waffenrock; **Bayer. 6.Infant.-Regt. Kaiser Wilhelm**. Soldat in Bluse; **Garde-Jäger-Bataillon**. Jäger im Waffenrock; **Jäger-Bat.Graf York v. Wartenburg (Ostpreuß.) Nr. 1**. Jäger in Bluse; **Bayer. 2.Jäger-Bataillon**. Jäger in Bluse.

Left to right: **Regt.d. Gardes du Corps**. Oberstleutnant im Waffenrock; **1.Garde-Dragoner-Regt**. Rittmeister in Bluse; **Garde-Kürassier-Regiment**. Major in Bluse; **2.Garde-Dragoner-Regt**. Oberleutnant im kleinen Rock.

Left to right: **1.Garde-Ulanen-Regt**. Leutnant in Bluse; **2.Garde-Ulanen-Regt**. Wachtmeister im Mantel; **3.Garde-Ulanen-Regt**. Unteroffizier in der Ulanka; **Leib-Garde-Husaren-Regt**. Gefreiter im Attila.

Uniforms and Equipment of the Imperial German Army 1900-1918

Left to right: **Kürassier-Regt. v. Seydlitz (Magdeb.) Nr. 7**. Wachtmeister im Waffenrock; **1.Brandenb. Dragoner-Regt. Nr. 2**. Leutnant in Bluse; **Königs-Ulanen-Regt. (1.Hann.) Nr. 13**. Ulan in der Ulanka; **Jäger-Regt. z. Pferde Nr. 2**. Leutnant im Waffenrock.

Uniforms and Equipment of the Imperial German Army 1900-1918

Left to right: **1.Leib-Husaren-Regt. Nr. 1**. Wachtmeister in Bluse; **Ulanen-Regt. König Wilhelm I (2.Württemb.) Nr. 20**. Leutnant im kleiner Rock; **K.Sächs.Karabinier-Regt. (2. schweres Regt.)**. Rittmeister im Waffenrock; **Bayer. 4.Chevauleger Regt. König**. In Bluse.

Left to right: **Garde-Pionier-Batallion**. Leutnant im Waffenrock; **Pionier-Bat Fürst Radziwill (Ostpr.) Nr. 1**. Pionier in Bluse; **Flieger-Bataillon Nr. 2**. Leutnant in Bluse; **Kraftfahr-Bataillon**. Unteroffizier in Bluse.

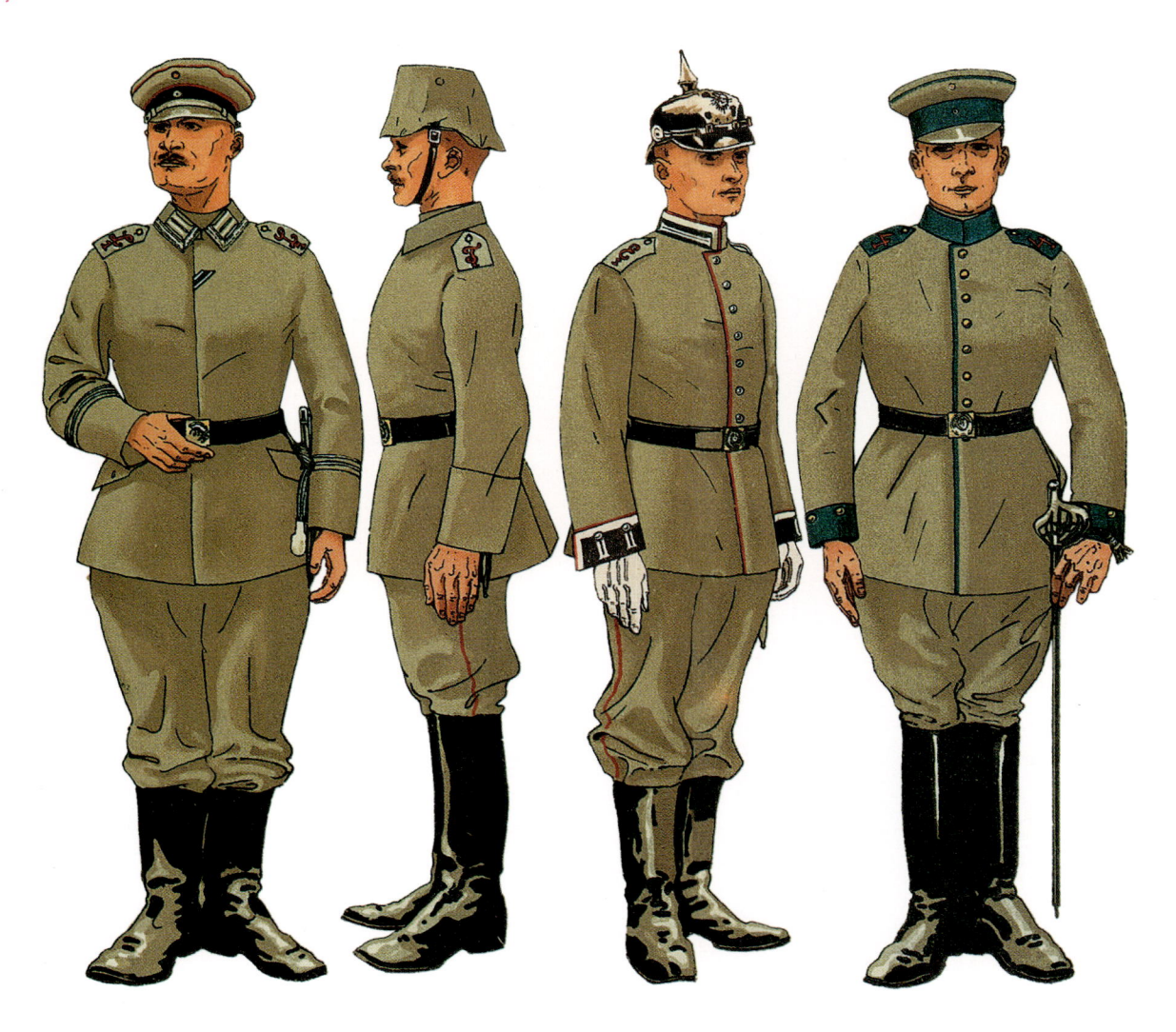

Left to right: **Luftschiffer-Bataillon Nr. 1**. Feldwebel in Bluse; **Telegraphen-Bataillon Nr. 2**. Soldat in Bluse; **Eisenbahn-Regt. Nr. 1**. Unteroffizier im Waffenrock; **Magdeb. Train-Abteilung Nr. 4**. Trainsoldat im Waffenrock.

Uniforms and Equipment of the Imperial German Army 1900-1918

Left to right: **2.Garde-Feldart.-Regt**. Hauptmann im Waffenrock; **3.Garde-Feldart.-Regt**. Leutnant im kleinen Waffenrock; **1. Pomm. Feldart.-Regt. Nr. 2**. Fähnrich im Waffenrock; **Bayer. 3. Feldart.-Regt. Prinz Leopold**. Unteroffizier in Bluse.

Uniforms and Equipment of the Imperial German Army 1900-1918

Left to right: **K. Sächs. 8. Feldart.-Regt. Nr. 78**. In Mantel; **2. Württ. Feldart.-Regt. Nr. 29**. Unteroffizier in Bluse; **Garde-Fußartillerie-Regt**. Leutnant in Bluse; **Bad. Fußartillerie-Regt. Nr. 14**. Hauptmann in Bluse.

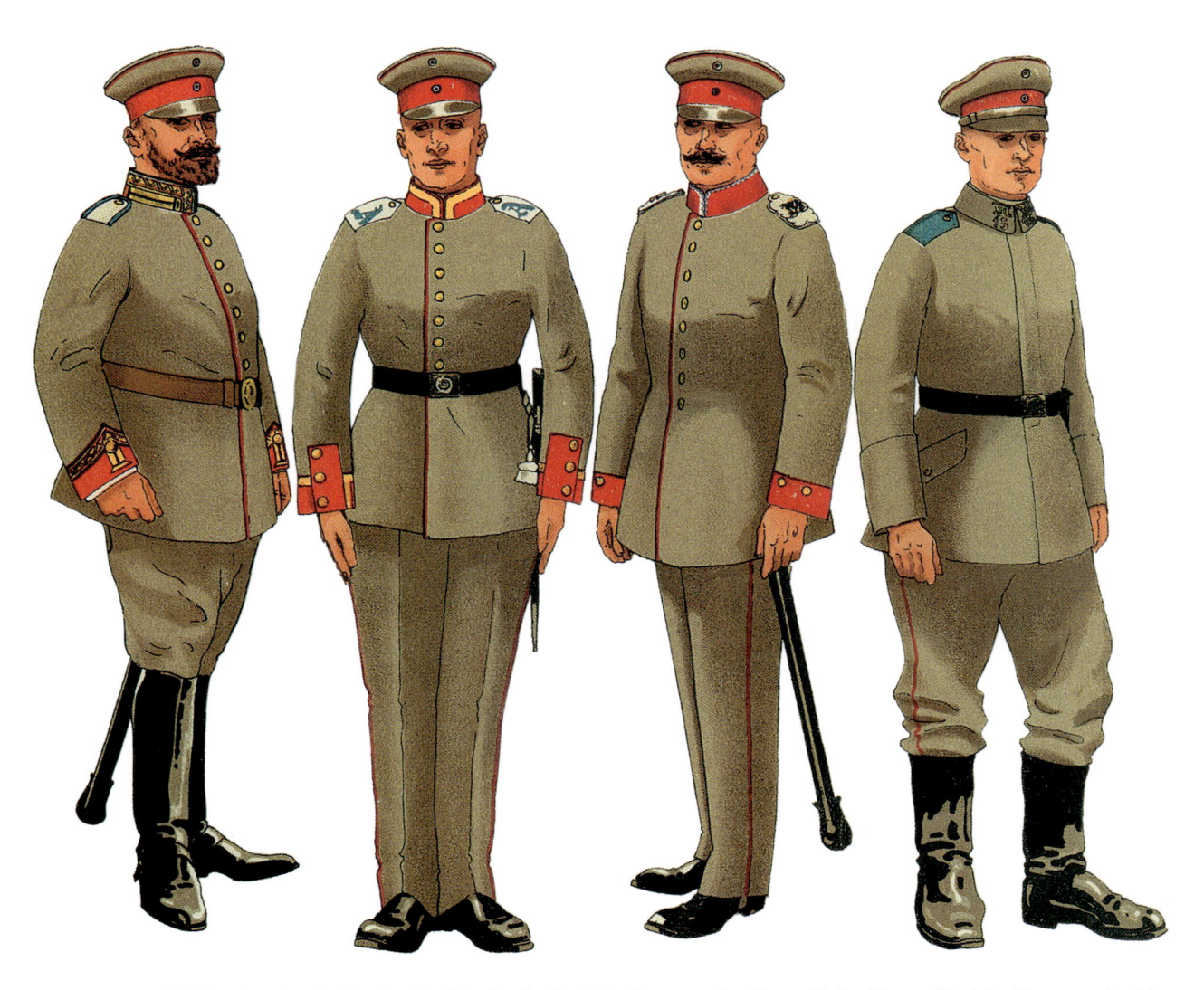

Left to right: **Offizier der Garde-Landwehr-Kavallerie**; **Bezirks-Kommando**. Unteroffizier; **Bayer. Bezirks-Kommando**. Major v.d. Landwehr-Insp. München; **Landsturm-Infanterie**. (from Landsturm-Inf.-Bat. Recklinghausen VII. 15.).

Left to right: **Soldat v. Bekleidungsamt des Gardekorps; Kadett (Selektaner); Unteroffizierschule Potsdam; Unteroffizier-Vorschule Wohlau**.

Uniforms and Equipment of the Imperial German Army 1900-1918

Left to right: **Reitendes Feldjägerkorps**. Im Waffenrock; **Feldgendarmerie**. In Bluse; **Leibgendarmerie I. Zug**; **Leibgendarmerie. II. Zug**. (Leibgarde der Kaiserin).

Left to right: **Krankenträger**; **Militär-Krankenwärter**. Im Waffenrock; **Halbinvaliden-Abteilung des Gardekorps**.

Uniforms and Equipment of the Imperial German Army 1900-1918

Left to right: **Generalarzt**. Im Waffenrock; **Stabsarzt**. In Bluse; **Stabsveterinär**. Im Waffenrock; **Kriegsgerichtsrat**. In Bluse.

Left to right: **Wirkl.Geh.Kriegsrat.**; **Intendanturrat**. Im Waffenrock; **Stabsapotheker**. Im Waffenrock; **Feldgeistlicher**.

Uniforms and Equipment of the Imperial German Army 1900-1918

Left to right: **Feuerwerksoffizier**. In Bluse; **Festungsbauoffizier**. Im Waffenrock; **Waffenmeister**. Im Waffenrock.

Uniforms and Equipment of the Imperial German Army 1900-1918

Left to right: **Oberzahlmeister**. In Bluse; **Unterzahlmeister**. In Bluse; **Armee-Musikinspizient**. In Bluse; **Garnisonverwaltungs-Beamter**. In Bluse.

Glossary

Adler: Eagle, Manufacturer of a one cylinder military motorcycle.
Aesculapius Staff: Insignia for the Medical Corps. Same in most nations.
Alpenkorps: Corps of those who served in the Alps.
Armeeflugpark: Army Flying Field
Attila: Jacket worn by Hussars with frogging on the front

Bergmütze: A mountain or ski cap with a short billed visor
Bluse or Feldbluse: The 1915 Model tunic for wear in the field
Bortenbesatz or Borte: Decorative uniform braid or tape
Brandenburg cuff: Uniform cuff having three buttons placed horizontally
Brief-stempel: Regimental postmark
Brotbeutel, or Breadbag: A cloth bag issued for carrying food items, including bread.

Carte-de-Visite: A small sized photograph mounted on a cardboard stiffener.
Chapka or Tschapka: Ulan helmet with a flat mortarboard top.
Chavauleger: Bavarian light cavalry.
Cuirassier or Kürassier: Heavy cavalryman who wore an armored chest plate, or a cuirasse.
Cypher: A regimental monogram or insignia.

Degen: Sword
Dienstpflicht: Regular military service
Dienstmütze: Service cap
Dux: Manufacturer of Army staff cars
Drachenballoon: A hanging balloon on a cable equipped with an observers basket for artillery spotting.

Einjahrig-Freiwillige: One-year volunteer

Fähnrich: Ensign, or Officer aspirant
Farrier: Army horseshoer
Fangschnür: Lines to secure cavalry headgear
Feldwebel: Sergeant
Feldwebelleutnant: NCO rank next to officer grade
Feld-und-Friedens: Field and peacetime uniforms
Feldgrau: Field gray uniform color adopted as early as 1907

Feldpost: Army postal service
Feldpoststempel: Field Post Office identity mark
Feldartillerie: Field artillery, horse drawn
Feldabzeichen: Field badge worn on headgear indicating state of origin
Fernglas 08: Binoculars Model 1908
Fernsprech: Telegraphist
Festung: Fortress
Flak: Anti-aircraft gun
Fuesschaenen: Harnesses, or tighteners for jackboots
Furchtlos und true: Württemberg motto "Fearless and true"
Fausthandschule: Woolen mittens
Feldkannone: Field cannon of lighter calibers
Feldkoppel: Leather field belt
Friendens uniform: Peacetime, or parade uniform

Garde Regiments: Elite regiments of all arms who wore special garde litzen on their uniforms
Garde litzen: Special tape strips worn on the cuffs and collars indicating a garde elite regiment
Gefreiter: Lance corporal
Gott mit Uns: Prussian motto mostly found on belt buckles. "God with us"
Gew 71., 71/84., 88., 98.: The designations for the basic German issue rifles Gewehr meaning rifle Model 1871, Gewehr Model 1871/ with 1884 modifications, Gewehr Model 1888 and Gewehr Model 1898
Gurtfuller 16: Device for loading ammunition belts

Halstuch: Neck liner to prevent chafing from the uniform collar
Hauptmann: Rank of Captain
Haarbusch: Parade plume made of horsehair
Hirschfänger: Hunting cutlass

Infanterie: German spelling for infantry
In True Fest: Motto found on Bavarian belt buckles. "In trust we holdfast"

Jäger: Literally, hunter. Jäger troops were skilled riflemen as were the Schützen

Jäger zu Pferde: Light cavalry, or mounted Jägers
Junger Regimenter: Junior, or newly formed regiment
Joppe Bluse, or tunic: Joppe means jacket, so this refers to a jacket styled tunic

Kokarde: A circular insignia worn on the cap or helmet with varying colors designating the state of origin of the unit
Koenigspreis 1913: A shooting prize awarded to units by the Kaiser for outstanding marksmanship. Awarded to the infantry, artillery, machine gun, Jäger and Schützen units.
Kar 88: Karabiner, or carbine (short rifle) Model 1888. Models of 1871, 1871/84, 98 and 98A were in use during this period.
Karpathenkorps: A mountain or Gebirgs Corps who served in the Karpathen Mountains area
Kannonier: Artilleryman

Koller: A tunic worn under the body armor used by the Garde du Corps and Cuirassier cavalry units.
Korporalschaft: Instructional training unit, or barracks squad
Kraftfahrer: Driver of a motorized vehicle

Landsturm: Home guard units, older reservists
Landwehr: Reserve, or land defense units.
Ledergamasche: Leather leggins worn with high top shoes or 3/4 laced boots
Lebel M 1893: French, first rifle to use a 8 mm smokeless powder cartridge. This and the Mannlicher Berthier M1907/15 were the most commonly used French shoulder arms.
Litewka: A loose service jacket, fly fronted with gathered cuffs
Litzen: Decorations of yellow or white tape found on the collar and cuffs of Garde, Füsilier, Grenadier, and other designated regiments
Luftschifftruppen: Air Service troops

MG 08: Standard Maxim heavy machine gun, model of 1908
MG 08/15: Light machine gun developed from the MG 08
Maschinengewehr: Machine gun
Minenwerfer: Trench mortar

NSU Heersmodel: Army model belt driven motorcycle produced by NSU

Offizierstellvertreter: Deputy officer, highest NCO rank

Paletot: Overcoat
Patronenkaste: Machine gun ammunition case, or box
Patronentasche: Infantryman's ammunition box normally of leather
Pelzmütze: Fur cap, or busby worn by Hussars
Perlring: A decorative ring at the base of the spike on the pickelhaube seen on officers helmets, only after the 1880s
Pferdeführer: Horse leader, or handler
Pickelhaube: Dress helmet with a spiked, or ball top
Pioniertruppen: Troops used for construction of bridges, trenches, fortifications, railways and military structures
Pour-le-Mérite: Nicknamed "The Blue Max", the highest Prussian bravery award to officers given in World War I
Portapee: Sword knot

Providentiae Memor: Found on Saxon belt buckles. Motto of the ruling Wettin family and came into use circa 1888

Quillback: A term describing the shape of a blade as in the case of the S98 bayonet

Radfaher: Cyclist
Raupenhelm: Bavarian style helmet with a fur comb running from back to front. Literally, caterpillar helmet
Rebatte: Regimental identifying colored fabric worn on parade on the Ulan lance cap, or on the breast of the Ulan tunic
Reichsrevolver: The Model 1883 revolver issued to the Army prior to the P. 08, or Luger
Reithose: Riding trousers, or pantaloons
Rittmeister: Cavalry rank equal to captain

Schlittenlafette: Sled-mount for the MG 08
Schneeschuhtruppen: Literally, snowshoe troops used in winter and mountain areas
Schnürschuh: Laced ankle high boots
Schützenschnar: Shoe, or boot harness for tightening the fit
Schwalbennester: Swallow's nest striped shoulder insignia worn by musicians
Schwarzlose M 7/12: Standard machine gun of the Austrian Army
Schwere Reiter: Heavy Cavalry, Saxon
Shako: A visored, tapering, conical helmet worn by Jäger, Schützen, Flieger, Machine Gun, and Landsturm troops
Spaten: Entrenching shovel
Speiss: Slang term for the 1st Sergeant
Strohhut M1900: A tropical issue straw hat model of 1900. Seen worn by Colonial troops in Africa and China

Totschläger: Spring-loaded English trench fighting club
Trauerband: A black mourning band
Tresse or Tressing: Decorative tape binding on cuffs and collars
Troddel: A bayonet knot designating company number
Trunnions: Cannon barrel pivot, or attaching points to the mount, or carriage
Tschapka: Lancer, or Ulan helmet
Tuchhose: Trousers

Ulanka: Tunic worn by Ulans, having two rows of seven buttons on the front
Unteroffizier: NCO

Vizefeldwebel: Rank of Vice Sergeant

Wachmeister: Highest Cavalry ranked NCO
Waffenrock: Dress tunic
Winker Abzeichen: Signaler's insignia

Yataghan Blade: A distinctive gentle "S" curved bayonet, or knife blade

Zahlmeister: Paymaster
Zielfernrohr 12: Optic sight for the MG 08

Further Reading

A Recommended Annotated Bibliography for Further Study

The following annotated bibliography is included to give the reader some insight into the many good, as well as adequate sources for further information on the Imperial German Army 1900-1918. The author has chosen to list the title first in the hopes that it will make the list easier to use. This may cause a hue and cry from the purists of form, but in any event, here's the list, and the comments are my own.

Die Uniformen der Deutschen Armee. Verlag von Moritz Ruhl, Leigzig 1914 edition. 31 colored plates of schematic uniform drawings, shoulder straps, and epaulets. 48 pages of text, 16 pages of regimental assignments by Armee Korps. 14 pages of garrison town listings. This work covers the blue M1895 uniforms with only minor mention of the Feldgrau uniforms.

Wandtaleln über die neue Felduniform der Deutschen Armee. 8 lithographed colored plates 42 x 52 cm drawn by Major Arthur Schmidt, Infanterie-Regiment Nr. 172. Published by Moritz Ruhl, Leipzig 1914. The M1910 uniform for enlisted personnel only is covered in this work. The style and color of these plates are outstanding.

Uniformenkunde Das Deutsche Heer, 3 volumes by Herbert Knötel d. J., Paul Pietsch, and Major a. D. Baron Colas. W. Spemann, Stuttgart 1982. Vol 1, 452 pages of text and black and white illustrations in text. Vol II, 122 color plates of Generals, Infantry, Jäger and Schützen, MG Abteilingen, and Cavalry. Vol. III, Plates 123-202 Artillery, Train, Specialized Troops, Pioneers, Landwehr, Sanitary, Marine Infantry, Colonial, Insignia and equipment. This is the best study made of late 19th century pre-war uniforms and equipment.

Deutschlands Armee in feldgrauer Kriegs-und Freidens-Uniform, by Oberstleutnant a. D. Freiherr N. d. Osten-Sacken v. v. Rhein, with 32 color plates by the military artist Paul Casberg. Published by P. M. Weber, Verlag, Berlin 1916. 36 pages of text with illustrations of accessories and buttons, 8 pages of black and white line drawings of insignia and uniform designs, 23 color plates of uniforms and insignia, 1 plate of uniform material, piping, and borte colors, and eight schematic regimental uniform and cap illustrations of Prussian, Baden, Hessian, Bavarian, Saxon and Württemberg variations. This covers only the M1915 uniforms.

Die Deutsche Armee in ihren neuen Feld-und Friedens-Uniformen. 93 colored lithograph illustrations of the M1915 uniform for all ranks and branches. 41 pages of descriptive text, illustrations by Paul Casberg, Verlag von Moritz Ruhl, in Leipzig 1916. This is a very complete work of all uniform variations in which the illustrations are more pleasing and clearly presented than those by the same artist in the previously mentioned volume and are reproduced in this second volume of the series.

Die Formations-und Uniformierungs-Geschichte des preussischen Heeres 1808-1914. Two volumes by Paul Pietsch, Verlag Helmut Gerhard Schulz, Hamburg 1963. This is the ultimate over-all history to date and covers the Prussian army in detail from 1808-1914. Volume one has four color plates of uniforms and many fine detailed black and white full page and in-text drawings of uniforms equipment and weapons. This volume covers Foot Troops; Infanterie, Jäger, Schützen, Pioniere, and Landwehr and contains over 280 pages. Volume II, like Volume I, has four color uniform plates and many black and white full page and in-text drawings. The coverage of Volume II is Kavallerie, Artillerie, Train, Landwehr and Generalstab containing 357 pages. These two volumes are currently quite hard to locate and hopefully they will be reprinted.

Die feldgrau Uniformierung des deutschen Heers, 1907-1918. Two volumes, Jürgen Kraus, Biblio Verlag, Osnabrück,

1999. Volume I contains 512 pages, hundreds of black and white line drawings in text, 24 color pages of schematic uniform illustrations of the 1907, 1908, 1910, 1913, and 1915/16 field and peacetime models, and four color plates illustrating Saxon and Hessian field uniforms. Volume II contains 574 pages, hundreds of black and white line drawings of uniforms in text and 30 pages of wartime photographs. Volume I covers the uniforms, equipment and small arms of the infantry, jäger/schützen and MG truppen, while Volume II covers cavalry, artillery, pionier, work troops, telegraph, luftstreitkräfte, train, sanitary, veterinary, technical, feldgendarmerie, disciplinary, general staff, feldpost, and the volunteer automobile and motor boat corps. Without doubt, this new publication is the most complete coverage under one title of the field gray uniform and the personal equipment in use during World War I that exists. Kraus has combed every meaningful source from the original War Ministry official directives, to periodicals such as *Feldgrau, Zeitschrift für Heereskunde*, the short-lived *Das Sponton*, as well as the volumes by Pietsch, Knötel, Krickel, and Lange, Ruhl, and others, combining this widespread data into two packed volumes. A must for any serious student.

L'Armee Allemande en 1914, by Didier Lainé, Chromos Service, Paris 1984. 297 pages and printed in French, German, and English. As set forth in its foreword, the intent of the work is to be a glossary, by regiment, of helmets, gorgets, cartridge boxes, and epaulets worn by the officers of Germany's land armies. There are references to enlisted versions, but the high quality officers material is its main focus. Extremely fine color photographs accompany very well executed line drawings and schematics in this basically illustration focused book. Not a great deal on uniforms per se, but a valuable source on the pre-war material. This has been recently republished in France in soft cover.

Militaria, A Study of German Helmets & Uniforms 1729-1918 by Jan K. Jube, published by Schiffer Military History, West Chester, PA (now Atglen, PA) 1990. Originally published under the title *Militaria-Ein Bilderbuch für Sammler und Freunde alter Helme und Uniform*, by Podzun-Pallas Verlag, Friedburg 1987. 235 pages with fine color and black and white photographs and prints. The bulk of the coverage is the period of the 1870s to just prior to World War One. Not much on the feldgrau period, but still a nice broadbrush coverage of the more colorful periods of German military fashion.

Cuirassiers and Heavy Cavalry, Dress Uniforms of the German Imperial Cavalry 1900-1914. By D. S. V. Fosten, and published by Almark Publishing Co., Ltd., London, June 1973. The first in a series by Almark on the pre-World War I German Cavalry. 136 pages. 16 excellent color plates depicting caps, uniforms, standards, trumpet and kettledrum banners. 99 black and white photos of uniforms, helmets, and troops, plus numerous in-text drawings make this small volume an excellent reference on the subject.

Hussars and Mounted Rifles, Uniforms of the Imperial German Cavalry 1900-1914. By D. H. Hagger and published by Almark Publishing Co. Ltd. 1974. 96 pages, 16 color plates and numerous line drawings by D. S. V. Fosten and R. J. Marrion, plus 55 photographs. The emphasis of this small volume is on the Hussar units, with just some 14 pages on the Jäger zu Pferde. The second part of the series by Almark, it is a good quick reference, covers a goodly amount of detail, and for those without German skills, it, too, is in English.

Lancers and Dragoons, Uniforms of the Imperial German Cavalry 1900-1914 by R. J. Marrion in collaboration with D. S. V. Fosten and D. H. Haggar, Almark Publishing Co. Ltd., New Malden, Surrey, U. K. 1975. 128 pages, 16 color plates of uniforms, caps, standards, Lance Pennons and drum banners, 23 sets of in-text black and white drawings, and 98 photographs of varying clarity. The third in the study, this busy little book is crammed with lots of good information and helpful color plates.

Military Transport of World War I, Including Vintage Vehicles and Post-War Models. By Chris Ellis, illustrated by Denis Bishop. The Macmillan Company, New York, 1970. A British edition was published by Blandford Press, London. This was the second in a Macmillan series entitled *Mechanized Warfare in Color*, the first being *Tanks and Other Armored Fighting Vehicles 1900-1918*, also published in 1970. This volume contains 185 pages, with 169 colored drawings by Bishop which are pleasantly done in his unique style. The text is brief, but factual, and the only criticism is that more types should have been included.

The Devil's Paintbrush, Sir Hiram Maxim's Gun, by Dolf L. Goldsmith, Collector Grade Publications Incorporated, Toronto, Canada, 1989. 367 pages with copious diagrams and photo illustrations. The definitive treatment of Maxim machine guns from the earliest designs to the guns built in China as late as 1935. All one would need to know on the MG 08 and MG 08/15, the accessories, and the loading and unloading of the weapon. A highly recommended book on the German World War I machine gun.

German Warships of World War I, by J. C. Taylor, printed in England for Doubleday & Co., Inc., Garden City, NY, 1970. 224 pages, 122 black and white photographs of ships, with descriptions of all types employed by the Imperial German

Navy and the final disposition of each ship. A fine small reference book.

Unsere Marineuniform, 1816-1969, by J. Zienert, published by Verlag Helmut Gerhard Schulz, Hamburg, 1970. 451 pages, 5 color plates, 3 large folding plates with uniform details of the Imperial Navy, 1890-1918, plus hundreds of photographs, engravings and in-text illustrations. Zienert's treatment of the history of Naval uniforms is of the same high quality as Pietsch's two-volume work on the Army. Done with typical German efficiency, this is the ultimate reference on the German Navy.

The Jasta Pilots, Detailed Listings and Histories, August 1916-November 1918, by Norman Franks, Frank Bailey and Rick Duiven. Grub Street, London, 1996. 364 pages, 32 pages of photographs, black and white profile illustrations of Jasta aircraft and their colors, casualty list, and an A-Z listing of all German fighter aces. A book for the student of German Jasta (fighter) pilots, squadrons, and victory details; well-presented and rich in detail.

German Knights of the Air 1914-1918, The Holders of the Orden Pour-le-Mérite. By Terry C. Treadwell and Allen C. Wood, Brasseys, London, 1997. 208 pages, 180 photographs and the biographies of the 81 German airmen who won the coveted "Blue Max", or the "Pour-le-Mérite". A good addition to a World War I aviation library as it contains the complete "Pour-le-Mérite" story of the German Air Service in one volume. The sources used by Treadwell and Wood are somewhat vague as the bibliography quotes six recently published volumes, but the photos and the information presented are quite good.

Aviation Awards of Imperial Germany In World War. Five volumes published to date with Volume VI to be published in the fall of 1999. By Neal W. O'Connor and published by the Foundation for Aviation World War I, Princeton, New Jersey, with later volumes published by Flying Machines Press, Stratford, Connecticut, 1988-1998. Over 1,350 pages are included in the first five volumes, with thousands of photographs of medals, airmen, and aircraft. If medals and orders and their Imperial German Air Service recipients are of interest, this series is the finest source available.

The German Army 1914-18, text by D. S. V. Fosten and R. J. Marrion, color plates by G. A. Embleton, Osprey Publishing, London 1978. 40 pages, 8 color plates depicting 35 uniforms of the wartime period, and 37 photographs of varying quality complete the illustrations. Number 80 in the *Men-at-Arms* Series, it contains basic information, and Embelton's plates, per usual, are well-rendered.

Uniforms and Organization of the Imperial German Army 1900-1918, by F. J. Stephens and Graham J. Maddocks, artwork by Brian Fosten. Almark Publishing Co. Ltd., London 1975. 80 pages, 8 color plates depicting 12 uniforms, all but three of pre-war uniforms, 49 photographs and in-text line drawings of uniform details. As in the previously listed volume, this book hits the highlights of the make-up of the army, the function of the branches and the variation of headgear types and descriptions of the M1910 and M1915 uniforms.

The U. S. Army Military History Research Collection at Carlisle Barracks, PA 17013, published in 1975; a volume called *Special Bibliographic Series, Number 12, Volume I, The Armies of Austria-Hungary and Germany 1740-1914*. 277 pages paper bound which lists their holdings on that subject. An interesting bibliography listing many obscure titles on all military subjects and including periodicals which cover all periods through 1945.

NOTES

NOTES

NOTES

NOTES

NOTES

NOTES

NOTES

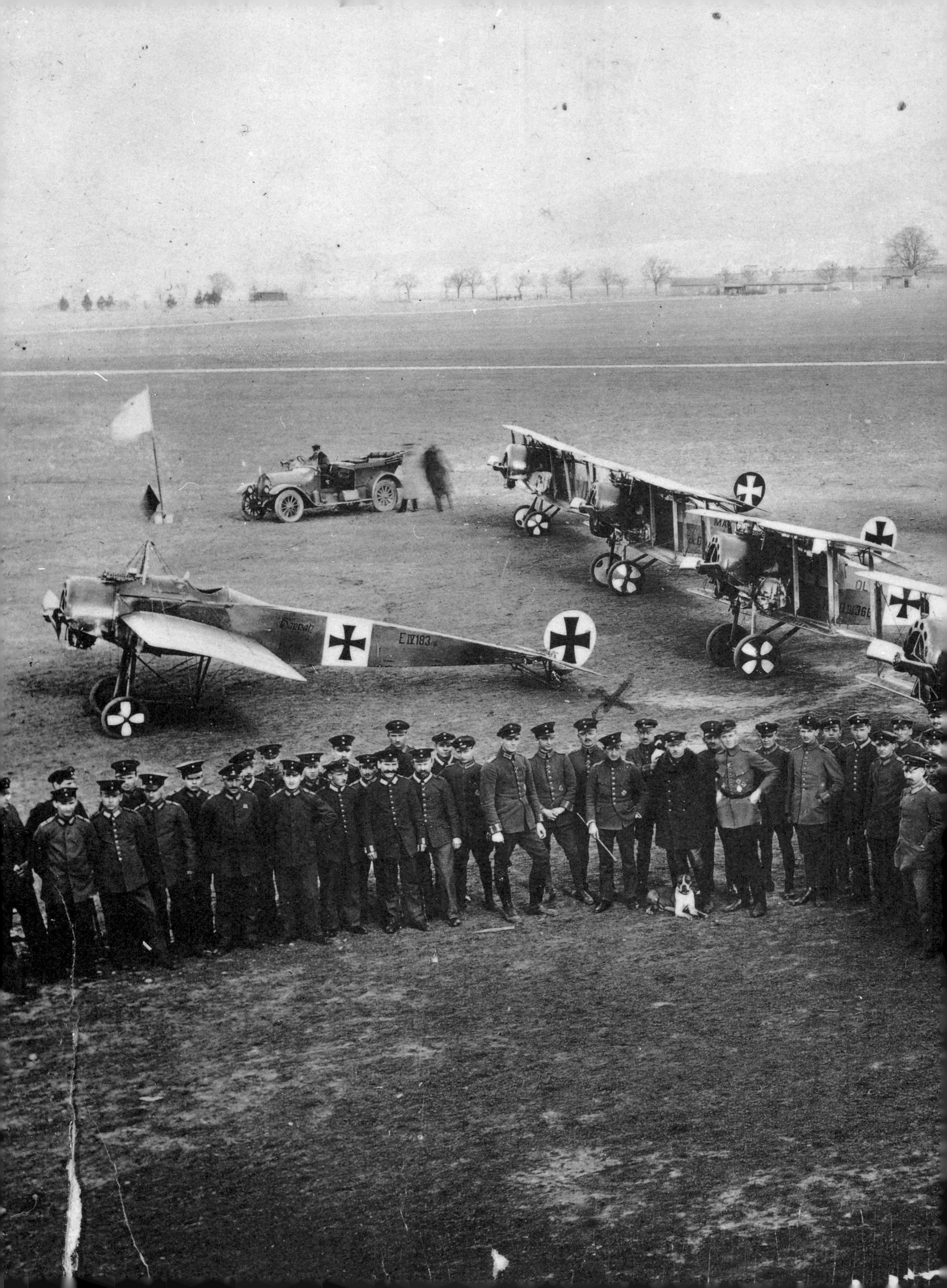